MW00800195

Mikel,
you're
awesome.

SQUELCHED

Thanks for all
that you do.

Terry

Squelched

Succeeding in Business and Life by Finding Your Voice

Terry Beard

Published by
Hybrid Global Publishing
301 E. 57th St., 4th floor
New York, NY 10022
www.hybridglobalpublishing.com

To contact the author go to: www.squelchedbook.com

Cover design by Joe Potter

ISBN: 978-1-948181-04-4

Printed in the United States of America

Contents

Part III: Speeches
A Sampling of Speeches Delivered at a Variety of Venues

Part IV: Letters to My Sons
Passing the Torch to the Next Generation

Preface

THE FIRST NINE MONTHS OF MY LIFE, I lived in a small, cramped space in my mother's womb. My escape from these confines came on June 30, 1947. A little later I existed in another small space, my attic bedroom, with small thinking all around me in the mill town in which I lived. I began to see wider horizons when, at age 12, I won a newspaper sales contest with the prize being a trip to Mexico City. My eyes were opened as a result of this trip and I began to glimpse the possibilities of escaping SmallVille, USA.

Here's how I remember it.

—Terry Beard

My Life as a Jigsaw Puzzle

MUCH OF THE OPPORTUNITY to build a good life is like assembling a thousand-piece jigsaw puzzle. We need to be able to piece the puzzle together to make a bigger picture. If there are missing pieces, it is tough to bring the big picture into focus. Sometimes we are not even aware that pieces are missing.

As we progress in our growth, we add more pieces to the puzzle and the picture becomes clearer. All of our lessons learned allow us to add more pieces to the big picture and obtain greater clarity and personal focus.

We hope that the lessons that emerge from this book become part of your effort and accomplishment in connection with clarification of your own big picture. May your world view become more focused and clearer as you progress through this book and add more pieces to the puzzle. As you read through and digest this book, you can enhance your personal guidance system, which will help you to sculpt your existence in keeping with your hopes and dreams. Enjoy the journey.

"It's difficult to turn the wheels of a parked car. But get it moving and you can guide it with just a touch. Whatever your dream, begin it. Boldness has genius, magic and power-steering in it. Release your brakes, begin now."—Unknown, quoted in *The Fieldbook of Team Interventions* and in *Journey to My Soul: Following Divine Navigations* (attributed to Edge Learning Institute)

Prologue: Not Good Enough!

THE DAY I FLUNKED OUT of Clark Junior College in Vancouver, Washington, was a life-sculpting event. During my first term in college, I was required to take a speech class. I knew that this challenge was do or die for me.

When my turn came to give my speech at Clark College, I stood at the dais to present my first speech since second grade.

In the second grade, I was not only the celebrated student body math whiz kid but I was asked to be the master of ceremonies at the student body assemblies. What an honor to be asked, as I was only in the second grade. I was told by my teacher that I was very good as a public speaker and was terrific with the microphone. I felt proud to be leading the school assembly for the entire student body. There were kids all the way through eighth grade sitting out in the audience.

I was on my feet as a public speaker. However, it was pointed out to me by the schoolhouse nuns that I had developed a rock 'n' roll attitude coupled with poor deportment. I was influenced by my idol Elvis Presley. I was exhibiting behavior unbecoming of a Catholic grade school student. In effect I was benched. I had lost my luster as potential student leader. I was labeled "a bad boy." Not good enough!

Being squelched and discouraged on an ongoing basis and by omission, a failure to encourage has a cumulative impact that gradually and steadily erodes our self-confidence and belief in our worth as a human being. When we don't feel good about ourselves, we have a difficult time standing up in front of others and withstanding the prospect of being judged and possibly found wanting. We often expect the worst from others if we think the worst of ourselves! We need "put ups" not "put downs" if we are to think well of ourselves and be ready to stand up to scrutiny. Whether we are young or when we are older, squelching erodes our confidence. What follows is a recollection of yet another "not good enough" message from when I was a student at Clark College.

I prepared my Clark College speech about my Oregon Journal newspaper-sponsored trip to Mexico City, and what the trip meant to me as a young lad growing up in Vancouver, Washington. I stood up to give my speech. I shook like I had never shaken before. I quaked in my boots. If I didn't pass muster at the podium I was surely going to soon be wearing combat boots, courtesy of being drafted into the US Army. I was totally embarrassed and humiliated in front of everyone. The words just wouldn't come, and I was petrified. The final blow came when the speech teacher said in front of the class, that in all of his years of teaching, I had given the worst speech he had ever heard in any of his classes. I realized that maybe he was right, my speech was not very good. Devastated. Immediately after being berated in front of everyone, I quietly left for the college bursar's office to withdraw from school. I asked for the refund percentage of tuition to which I believed I was entitled, but to no avail. I missed the deadline to receive a refund on my tuition by one day. I was in and out of college in less than four weeks. I was frightened, I was scared and discouraged, and I had no one to chat with, no one to console me, to guide me, to help me sort out my feelings, my life. I was alone.

Now out of school, with oodles of time in front of me, I began to ponder. I was sad, lonely, and pensive. What had caused me to choke up in front of others each time that I was on my feet to give a speech?

Everyone has encountered obstacles; personal and business difficulties to resolve whether at home, at work, or at play. While struggling with life's challenges whether as a second grader or a high school student, in college, in a relationship, or in a job, many of us have lost our way, lost our footing and stumbled. We get discouraged and demoralized, which fuels and aggravates our fear of public speaking.

Many of us have never had the opportunity, nor made the opportunity, to fully work through our life-squelching issues so we limp along living lives of quiet desperation. We remain speechless.

In the process of having my speaking wings clipped by the vicissitudes of life my shoes became filled with lead. I was so weighted down with discouragement and self-doubt, that I was reluctant to get back on my feet to speak, or give voice to what I really wanted to say to the folks with me and around me. I was lost, I had lost my voice.

As the years went flying by, I recognized more and more that I was not feeling good about myself. Not Good Enough. As much as I wanted to participate socially and to be accepted by others, whenever the spotlight shined on me, I made excuses to take my leave. If I knew that I was going to be called upon to speak, I opted out, either by not attending an event, hiding in the john until the opportunity passed, or having someone else do my speaking for me.

As the years wore on, as a result of being benched in the second grade, to nearly flunking out of high school to flunking out of junior college, I realized that I was stuck. Not feeling good about myself kept me weighted down and silenced, my blood pressure shot up, my anger soared and I created a hard crust to protect myself.

More and more, I began to realize that when you are emotionally wounded and fear speaking, you retreat into your inner fortress and develop a hard shell to fend off further hurt and discouragement. This shell often encases and locks away your buried treasure which are the riches that you have to share with the world. These treasures may remain locked away in a crusty vault of self-protection.

To overcome my fear of speaking, I realized I needed to go to work to unlock my personal treasure trove, enabling me to become unbound. Only then could I share my personal treasures with others.

Our transition from torment to mentor is our pathway and opportunity to help others conquer their personal fears. As we recover our sense of worth we are increasingly emboldened to reach out and connect with others and help them on their way. Joining hands with others enables us to do so much more than we can do alone. "Alone we can do so little, together we can do so much."

As I have reclaimed my self-esteem through learning how to become a public speaker through Toastmasters, I have developed the philosophy that our society needs to do much better with child rearing, human relations, and the art of mutual encouragement and celebration. Let's consider living a life of celebrating and encouraging human potential. Let's live in a Win-Win world and in the kind of world where we share mutual uplift with one another. That way we make sure that everyone gets a turn on the launch pad of life.

Shortly, after turning 50, I was encouraged by Dr. Richard to attend Dale Carnegie Speaking Seminars, which turned out to be a safe harbor place of encouragement for me. As a result, I fell in love with public speaking, and found many friendships which in the past would have eluded me. At Dale Carnegie, I felt like a kid in a candy store with lots of money.

After graduating from the Dale Carnegie Seminars, Wake Mack, a member of the Arlington Club invited me to join Toastmasters. I accepted the invitation to become a Toastmaster. I found an opportunity to peck my head all the way out of the protective shell in which I had been living. The public speaking opportunities which accrued then and to this day have helped me to be on the dance floor of life and dance like nobody is watching, Toastmasters has helped me define and redefine myself in an uplifting way.

My journey from living in fear of speaking to standing up to speak with confidence will hopefully inspire and motivate readers to work through self-esteem and self-doubt issues to live a happier and a more meaningful and fulfilling life by finding your voice. I am sharing my journey so as to inspire you to recognize that through self-development and public speaking you can reclaim the power of your voice.

Through the process of giving speeches, and overcoming the fear of public speaking in a safe harbor such as Toastmasters, the benefits and rewards are awesome. Each day, I am full of gratitude for having taken the risk to overcome my glossophobia … fear of public speaking.

Today, more than ever, the world needs a wakeup call. In the course of life people get a job, many marry and some have children. We continue to hop on the common conveyor belt of life without taking the time to grow and develop ourselves, and resolve the "fear of public speaking." We prance along in life like sheeples on the way to the feeding pen.

In school, we are required to learn how to read, to write, and do arithmetic, to graduate. Too few of us are required to learn the art of public speaking. This needs to change!!!

To change the collision course I was traversing in my life, I took the risk to rise above my fear of public speaking and learned to speak effectively and confidently. Learning to speak in public has made a huge difference in my life. I resolved my family multi-generational legacy of the fear of public speaking. I have not only created a cornucopia of opportunity in my life, my two sons, Jeff and MG, have found their voices as well. I found, as I hope you will, that the key to freedom is within our grasp. "We just need to take the first step even if we do not see the whole staircase." (Martin Luther King)

My personal story is everyone's story, the fear of public speaking. Most of us would rather die than be called upon to give a speech. The people who are frightened to stand up to speak suffer from a lack of self-confidence and a fear of being judged. It is reputed that 80–90% of the population in the USA, suffers from glossophobia … the fear of public speaking. We can overcome this personal handicap. Read this book, apply the principles offered and you will be on your way to finding your voice!!

Part I

Squelched, How I Lost My Voice

Drafted US Army:

Continuing to Fight My Battles

As I HAD PREDICTED, I was no longer a student in college, the military draft notice came, and I was required to report to Fort Lewis on January 11, 1967. My fellow draftees and I were rounded up like cattle and loaded onto a bus without any personal baggage. A few long hours later, we arrived at our destination, boot camp, Fort Lewis, Washington, which is located a few miles north of Olympia. As we passed the Olympia off-ramp from the interstate highway, I was reminded of the night that my dad had bailed me out of jail only a few years prior.

Now that I had my freedom from college, and on the military dole, I was free of economic worries, I was questioning myself. Having earned poor grades in high school and without the possibility of earning a college degree, where was all of this leading me?

While serving in the US Army, I was essentially on a government sponsored vacation. I was lucky enough to have been shipped overseas to Germany, not to the war in Southeast Asia. The Viet Nam War was blazing across the television screen each night, with news anchor Walter Cronkite delivering all the news from around the world from his plush office in New York City. It was clear to me that I would be sent off to a war that no one understood, even in its early years. But as a US citizen and the son of a Navy veteran of World War II, I would of course serve my country.

Immediately upon arriving at Fort Lewis, I could identify with my idol Elvis Presley. My Elvis-styled hairdo was within 24 hours a thing of the past. Like everyone else, I was now sporting a white sidewalls haircut, which looked as if we were all right out of Terry's Barber School. Like everyone else, I was outfitted with a new wardrobe, given a duffle bag and foot locker, and assigned to a billet that bunked 55 raw recruits. My first job in basic training was to do my turn under the billet shoveling coal at 3 a.m. in the cold and freezing rain.

Actually, I enjoyed myself tremendously in basic training: all of the buck privates were readymade friends, and one's station in life didn't count. The biggest challenge of our daily grind was banding together to endure our arrogant and mouthy drill sergeant.

Frequently, we buck privates were told by our drill sergeant to drop to the ground, sometimes straddling a mud puddle, in the pouring rain, and to give him twenty push-ups. We may have thought we were developing our physical endurance but we were also bowing down to his highness.

Each week, right after we each received our weekly stipend in cash, our drill sergeant called us all to "attention" in the privacy of our barracks, and then after we all assembled in formation, we were ordered to be "at ease." We were then asked to make a donation to his weekend beer drinking and carousing fund. If we cooperated with him, he assured us that he would be busy over the weekend, and we'd be free of him harassing us. Eventually, after we graduated from basic training, we learned that our drill sergeant was demoted for his behavior and shipped to Viet Nam.

As buck privates, we were all given a battery of tests in the first few days of basic training. We were measured, sized-up, and ranked. Our test results became numbers affixed to our permanent military files. My poor high school grades didn't hinder my ability to score well on the military tests. I had one goal. I wanted a desk job in the military or else I would become a ground pounder or an artillery man. When asked questions on the multiple choice tests as to whether I liked the outdoors, or liked to work on cars, go hunting, or go for a walk in the woods, I responded, "No."

From my perspective, I did well on the tests. I was given a desk job, and was awarded a Military Occupation Specialty (MOS) 71F40 (Postal Clerk). Once I completed basic training, my next move in my military career was to attend Advanced Individual Training (AIT).

While I felt relieved about my MOS, I was harassed constantly by the senior military commanding officers at Fort Lewis. In the first couple of weeks during boot camp training, I was approached by a captain and a lieutenant on more than one occasion and urged to consider going to

Officer Candidate School (OCS) in Fort Benning, Georgia. I already knew that Fort Benning was famous for infantry training. No way. One of the captains became visually disgusted with me during the interview process, and he noted and underscored in my permanent file that I couldn't make a decision. I couldn't care less, because I knew saying "yes" to OCS was a free ticket non-stop to Viet Nam, everyone's biggest fear. I knew that if I was given orders to go to Viet Nam I could always delay my departure by saying yes, I'll go to OCS.

Once I graduated from basic training, I was shipped off to Fort Benjamin Harrison, Indiana, "The Home of the Army Dollar" (the military financial center). I spent six weeks at Fort Benjamin Harrison, where I learned how to run and operate an Army Postal Office (APO). My fellow Army buddies and I had the time of our lives. Every day we wore our dress blues … our Army-issued dress suits, with a shirt and tie. My first chance to play executive, all dressed up but nowhere to go except to work in the APO training school. After work, it was another matter; we were back in our khakis, our casual dress, and on the road again off base to chase the local chicks.

Finally, it was graduation day from AIT; I received my postal worker certification papers and my orders for my first tour of duty. To this day, I wonder why I was picked out of hundreds and hundreds of graduates to be the only Private First Class (PFC) who wasn't shipped to Viet Nam. I never had to play the "I'll go to OCS" card to delay my trip to Viet Nam. (I was learning to play "the game.")

Everyone else I met at basic training in Fort Lewis, and my fellow Army buddies at Fort Benjamin Harrison, believed that we were all going to be shipped overseas. With my "orders" to report to Frankfurt, I felt like I was off on a government-sponsored vacation for two years. Yes, I was the luckiest guy in the world; I had in fact just won the military lottery. Freedom and safety.

Once I had my overseas shipping orders, I could not get out of Fort Benjamin Harrison fast enough. Several of my Army buddies, friends for a season, resented my good fortune to be traveling east rather than west to Southeast Asia with them.

Free room and board in Deutschland. My new home was in downtown Augsburg at Infantry Kaserne, a few blocks from the Koenigsplatz, and not far from where I worked at APO 09112. Along with my Army postal buddies, I lived on the fourth floor overlooking the fringes of the city's center. We were provided with private rooms, some rooms with two guys to a room, and some spacious rooms with four guys to a room. I felt like we lived in a hotel except that the walls were Army green, which was a constant reminder that we were really in the military. The marble floors and the hardwood floors were spotless. I felt at home, while in the military. I had some ready-made friends, a few bucks in my pocket, drinking buddies, all of us with a common cause. Be good boys and appreciate the fact that we were not in the Mekong Delta or at My Lai.

Many months after my arrival at Infantry Kaserne, I asked a question of one of my senior officers. "What is it about that huge pile of brick and rubble at the corner of our building?" I was told that pile was yet to be scooped up; it was debris from World War II. Some twenty years later, Germany was still cleaning up after the devastation from the war. The Cold War had just begun.

My monthly Army stipend covered most of my toiletry needs and daily consumption of the world-famous German beer … Löwenbräu.

My stint in the military was awesome. Those guys serving their time in the military working as cooks or postal clerks had what we referred to as "dick" duty (easy). During times of war, mail call is #1 for all the troops, and during times of peace, it was #2 after chow at the mess hall. I thought I would rather be #2 in popularity in Germany than #1 in popularity in Viet Nam.

The time passed quickly at Infantry Kaserne. We never had the regular Army protocol of reveille, as did other Army units at the Kaserne, nor did we have white-glove inspections of our barracks. We were completely free to do our own thing. Everybody wanted their mail, so we were left alone. I never felt so popular. While in high school, I was in a fight daily, and friends were scarce. In the Army, there was no fighting, no class struggle, and your grades in high school or your parents' wealth made no difference. We all got along well and we all wore green, the great leveler.

We worked five and one half days a week. After work, our evenings were ours to do as we wished. My fellow postal Army buddies and I recognized that we were fortunate to be living peacefully in the heart of Europe.

The day I arrived in Augsburg, I looked out the window and spotted across the street the local disco, called the Rumpel Kammer ("junk house"), which I soon learned was off limits to GIs. The noise of this joint on the weekends reminded us of the fun we were missing back home with our girlfriends.

Looking out the window and a block down the street from the Rumpel Kammer, I saw a German *gasthaus*, which wasn't off limits to GIs. It wasn't long after I started frequenting this pub that I met Lisa Bremer. Lisa was recently divorced from an American military officer and was looking for a little fun to wriggle her way out of boredom and loneliness. Well, she found it. She became my girlfriend, my big sister, and my mother all in one nice package. Often after a few beers, I would ride along with her in her car to make the trip to the outskirts of town to sleep overnight in a little garden shack no larger than 125 square feet. The one room was outfitted with a small table and two chairs, a little sink, and a tiny bed that allowed two people to snuggle. What else was needed? In the mornings, it was easy to get dressed and go back to work. We wore the same Army fatigues, so even though those fatigues from the night before might be a little wrinkled, who cared? I wasn't out of uniform.

Lisa was 36 years old when we met, I was 20, and to this day many decades later we are still connected as friends. She looked after me while I lived down the street from her apartment. She bought a car for me and my Army buddies, and my buds and I drove all over Bavaria. At the end of each month, she would always make sure that I had money for a little gas, liters of beer, and a ticket or two to the flicks at the PX. Most importantly, she always invited me to her family dinners on Bismarckstrasse, two blocks from the Kaserne. I obliged. I was one lucky guy; few of my Army buddies had a German home to call their own.

While serving on active military duty in Europe, I traveled extensively. I took over eight weeks of real vacation and lived life to the fullest.

One trip that I'll never forget was going to Scandinavia. I had heard that Sweden was the land of free love. It was a goal of mine to experience this dream. One night, at the Britannia Inn, in the heart of Copenhagen, I was playing darts, a game called 301. After drinking several beers, I struck up a conversation with a cute girl who lived 30 minutes outside of Copenhagen. A dream was fulfilled, to go home with a Swedish or a Danish girl. The following morning, I woke up in her bedroom, and as we opened the bedroom door, we were immediately in the kitchen. We joined her parents at the breakfast table. As I sipped my coffee and reflected over the experience of the last 12 hours, I thought, "I'm living the dream."

The following day, I left for Stockholm. At the train station, I bought a paperback book that one would never see back home at the newsstand. The book was entitled *Flossie*. I was so excited to read this sex and trash–filled book that I began to read excerpts of it out loud to my travel buddy, Gary Walden. As the train continued to chug along, I kept on reading the juicy pieces to Gary. We were sharing our trip from Copenhagen to Stockholm with three other travelers, local gals our age who were as cute as little buttons. Finally, one gal said to me, "We understand English." In a New York second, I turned red, too embarrassed to speak, and I bolted to another cabin. I lost any opportunity for us to hook up with these gals upon our arrival in Stockholm. Sex might be out in the open in this part of the world but being discreet was expected. This time I was benched for the right reasons. Lesson learned.

It is during these years in the military that I learned the thrill and excitement of European travel. I fell in love with Paris.

In December 1968, I was honorably separated from the US Army; like the rest of the troops during this period we received our discharge papers some six years later after our separation date. At the time of separation, we knew that we might be called back into active duty, given that there was a war going on in Southeast Asia.

I could go on and on about my time on my government-sponsored two-year vacation in the US military, but now I knew that I was ready to go to school once I was separated from the US Army, and make something of my life.

Army Reflections: Time to Reflect

HURRY UP AND WAIT. There was ample time to ponder during my government sponsored vacation. Night after night, I would climb into my assigned bunk exhausted.

I reflected on the life path which I had traversed over the last nineteen years. Why had I made the choices that I had made to earn a government sponsored two-year stint as a draftee in the military, and to subject myself to the beck and call of Uncle Sam. US Government Property; US 56 931 583

If I had been more studious in school, been a good boy, good enough, I would have been able to avoid the draft and eight weeks of army boot camp at Ft. Lewis, WA., in the dead of a rainy winter.

With lots of time on my hands, in boot camp riding around in a convoy going to and from the rifle range, doing push-ups, or peeling potatoes in the mess hall, I began to reflect on my past.

In 1946, shortly after my father Lew, a World War II veteran was discharged, he married my mother Elaine, at Holy Redeemer Catholic Church in Portland, Oregon. Months after the wedding they moved to Mt. Morris, Illinois, to live near my father's family, in search of family support and a job.

On June 30, 1947, a hot, humid day, I made my debut, son number one, in a farm village in Oregon, Illinois, an hour and a few minutes west of Chicago, along the Rock River. The temperature was well over 100 degrees. There was no air conditioning … yes, it was a hot start, and each year on my birthday I was always reminded by my mother of the hot weather and what heat I generated coming out of the chute. My dad was 22 years old when I was born, and my mother was turning 20. Kids were having kids. My dad had not gone past the third grade and there were few books around the house, a storybook or two, but with three young boys to feed and no money available for anything other than food, clothing, and shelter, education or discussion was something that my parents didn't have time for. They did their best but when there is nothing in the cupboard there is little to put on the table.

In 1948, during my toddlerhood, my parents moved from Illinois to Vancouver, Washington, where we rented a cozy, prefabricated World War II project home which was less than 500 square feet in total. In our cozy home we became quickly a family of five: my parents and their three sons, Terrill, Darrell (known as Eddy), and Errol (known as Mike). My mother had her heart set on her first child being a daughter, whom she planned to name Cheryl. When I was born, I was named Terrill, as the name rhymed with Cheryl. Disappointed again about not having a girl, my mother continued her rhyming fest and named her second son Darrell, after a famous baseball player, and the third son Errol, after my mom's favorite movie star, Errol Flynn. Finally, she gave up on having a girl and named her fourth son Gary.

By the age of three, I had already experienced a few memorable scenarios, which are my pre-kindergarten memories. One very chilly Sunday morning, approaching my third birthday, as we were warming up the car preparing to go to church, my father ran into the house, leaving me at the wheel. "I can do this," I thought as I contemplated becoming a chauffeur. I had been told to sit in the car while my dad refilled the tea kettle with boiling water to melt the ice on the front and back windows of our family's 1941 Oldsmobile Coupe. While I was waiting, curiosity overcame my boredom as I began to explore and fiddle with the car's stick shift and the brake and gas pedals. Suddenly, I had engaged the car's reverse gear and then in a flash I backed up the family auto and succeeded in wiping out nearly 100 feet of picket fence. Uh-oh, there goes our dog Spot on the run. Spot escaped being hit by the car and he remained cool. I only wished that my parents would have remained as calm. Needless to say, it was a quiet ride to church. I felt accomplished; I knew how to make things happen. I liked driving the 1941 Oldsmobile Coupe, usually; admittedly I did a better job when I sat on my father's lap. My dad would control the gas and brake pedals while I took my turn at the steering wheel. Beep, beep, here I come!!

At three or four years of age, as I was watching from my dad's shoulders, we were standing in our fenced-in backyard, and a pickup truck blasted through the intersection, flipping on its side. The truck blew up, flames shot skyward, and two men jumped out. As we learned later, a little boy burned to death in that accident. My feelings ran deep: Why did they not get that kid out? I don't want my dad to lose me like that!

At age four, nearly every day in our newly fenced yard, I played with my two brothers out behind the house. On one beautiful and uneventful Saturday afternoon, a space in the shade behind the house out of Mom's sight allowed me to cut my brothers' hair. I became the family barber. Mom always knew we were up to something when it was quiet in the backyard. This one Saturday, she came outside to inspect. Seeing that Brother Mike's haircut was finished and Brother Eddy's was in process, Mother exclaimed, "What is going on?"

"Mom, Dad's working swing-shift today, somebody's got to prepare us for church tomorrow … "

When Dad returned at midnight, we were all awake to greet him because we had some unfinished family business. Yep, my bottom was warmed up again, squelched for taking initiative. At church, for all to see, we three brothers had been to Terry's backyard barber college, where our ears had been lowered. I imagine we were a family to behold: Mom, Dad, and us three brothers—Ed, Mike, and me! As always, we sat in the second pew on the Gospel side at St. Joseph's Church. My parents never told us but I knew that it was easier for all of us to pray and pay attention to the church service when we were sitting up front. This seating arrangement orchestrated by my parents had forced the priest giving the sermon to keep his scolding eyes on the Beard boys, serving as a free babysitting service.

"You three boys look great, today," commented family friend Margaret Carson, as she winked at me with her sparkly eyes and wide smile. Mrs. Carson always sat directly in front of us. She never had any children, and my best guess is that she enjoyed playing auntie to me and my brothers.

I asked, "Mrs. Carson, do you like our haircuts?"

"You guys are so handsome."

"Thanks, Mrs. Carson."

"See, Mom, Mrs. Carson likes our haircuts."

Mrs. Carson was one of the first angels in my life. Times were difficult for my parents and having three boys full of piss and vinegar added to their already difficult situation. Mrs. Carson winked and smiled all the time at the three of us. She lightened the church-day load of discipline that we were receiving from our well-intentioned parents as part of the aftermath of my haircuts. To my mom's dismay, all during the Sunday mass, my buttons were popping from my good-looking Sunday duds, but to no avail: my bottom was warmed up after church. I tried to convince my mom that Mrs. Carson loved our haircuts, but it didn't prevent me from receiving another penance, a punishment.

At age four, it became my duty to go to the local grocery store for my mother and always I came up a few cents short when I arrived at the checkout counter. I was barely able to see across the counter without standing on my tiptoes. Talk about a comeuppance—I was learning the meaning of the word before I was able to comprehend or read it. So on each trip to the grocery store I would have to ask for a small loan from the grocery clerk. Each time I returned for my next shopping outing, I first went to the counter to settle up the outstanding debt. I was so embarrassed when I did not have enough money to pay for groceries that I'd grab the stuff after promising to pay the loan with a mutual wink and nod of our heads. Then I would run out of the store and run home as fast as I could, hoping that no one would see me. I already knew that I was living in survivor mode, and there was no one to talk to about my situation, so I began to deny my feelings. I couldn't talk to my parents either as it would only hurt their feelings more to be reminded that they were poor. I went all out to satisfy Mom's desire to give us a bite to eat. I knew already that my parents were working hard to make ends meet. Each time I went shopping for Mom, I observed the goodies on the store's shelves and what others were buying. I wondered why we couldn't buy regular cow's milk and real maple syrup at the market like everyone else.

As a little tyke, I was always up early in the morning full of energy and ready to get the day going. The first stop was to hop into my parents' bed to snuggle up. Upon my jumping in the middle of my sleepy dad's back, he would immediately hand me his underwear with instructions to take his jockeys out to the living room and turn up the heat. Once the stove unit was at a comfortable temperature, I was instructed to put the shorts on top of the stove. Minute by minute, I would give my dad a blow-by-blow description of how warm his underwear was getting from the heated stove. Today, more than a half century later, I can only imagine what my folks were doing under the sheets. They were perhaps preparing or practicing for child number three or four, warming up the sheets in their own way. Sometimes it seemed like it took all morning for my dad to say that it was a good time for me to return to the bedroom with his hot jockeys.

Onion sandwiches were a preparation which my father shared with me for the first time when I was less than three or four years old. It was a ritual on those Sundays when Dad's work shift schedule allowed him to go to mass with Mom, my brothers, and me. Immediately upon returning from church, Dad and I would prepare onion sandwiches. I always asked my brothers if they would like any onion sandwiches and always the response was "No." Dad and I quietly prepared the onion sandwiches and ate them while waiting for my mother to serve us our weekly Sunday breakfast pancakes prepared with powdered milk and homemade syrup made out of boxed brown sugar.

The onion sandwiches are easy to make and yummy, but messy to eat. To this day, I eat onion sandwiches over the sink to save time and energy on clean-up. When indulging in these sandwiches, I always think of my dad, to whom I thought I was so close until I came into my own. As the years have rolled on, I have come to understand how we eventually became increasingly distant from one another.

Down the street from where we lived (with a rebuilt white picket fence), there was a guy living with his wife, let's call him Bert the jerk. He was college educated and a public school athletic director. From an early age, less than five years old, I could tell by the way this guy treated my father that he thought he breathed a little finer air than my dad. My father wasn't good enough. I could see it in Bert's eyes and I knew that dissing my dad was dissing me. Until the day I graduated from high school I had traffic with this pompous ass, much to my chagrin. I wondered why Bert seemed a little better than we were, but I could never put a finger on it until later. It takes a good person to be humble and kind around those who struggle. This guy used his body language to telegraph his feeling that we weren't good enough. Bert died at a very young age. I imagine he had his demons, too. His ongoing self-importance about his education and much higher level of income than my father's served to forge a divide between his family and ours and to remind me on numerous occasions that the Beards weren't good enough.

Bert bragged that he didn't have to serve his country in a military uniform, and suggested that he thought he was a little better than the rest of us. But Bert and his family felt they deserved to rent a WWII project home like the one my veteran father had earned. I learned in retrospect that humility is a desirable character trait.

In the spring of 1965, my senior year of high school, I had additional traffic with Bert, the horse's ass, a teacher in my high school. He was going to do a little makeup call that accomplished a mission. His goal was to see that I'd graduate from high school, but the style and process of what he did on makeup day I was to learn from my true friend Gary Huss. After Gary and I graduated from Hudson's Bay High School in the spring of 1965, I learned that if Bert wouldn't have me in his homeroom, I would not be able to graduate from high school. Gary explained to my classmates that Bert saw me as a trouble maker, a bad boy, and a disruptive force, but asked for my classmates' cooperation and understanding to get me through to graduation day. Not good enough and now also humiliated. Go Eagles! With Gary's help, I graduated 467 out of 505. I made it to the goal line!

Those first five years living in a war project home in the McLoughlin Heights east of Vancouver, Washington, were riddled with experiences that no doubt shaped my life. We lived in a clean home, had simple food, clean clothes, not fancy though, not a lot of extra heat but lots of blankets and a central coal-burning stove that became an oil stove propped up in our tiny living room. It was here in east Vancouver where I learned how to shop, how to borrow money, cut hair, drive a car, and learn via our parish church and our neighbors that that our family was poor and therefore not quite good enough. But it was also during these years that I learned to hustle and to make the most of the hand that was dealt to me. I developed creativity, boundless energy, true grit, and determination. Out of struggle grew determination.

In 1952, the year before we moved to our next home, I met another Bert, the Vancouver City bus driver. He was the best. Neatly dressed in his gabardine trousers, with a shirt and tie topped off with a bus driver hat, he became my friend. He always picked me up from the bus stop at the corner near our home and dropped me off at the front door to Providence Academy kindergarten. Bert was the nicest man, and was *an angel*. I felt tall with and around him. He always said nice things to me and to others, and my friendship with him made me feel like a million dollars. I enjoyed him so much, at times I would stay on the bus for an extra loop on his route just to stand up proudly next to him and play the assistant driver answering the questions of the passengers who needed help with directions and connections on his route. Bert, the bus driver, was my friend, and looking back this was one of the first places in which I was the recipient of caring and companionship from someone outside my family. Once we moved, I cried for weeks as a result of losing contact with him. Today, whenever I wear gabardine trousers I think of Bert; he was not only a spiffy dresser but someone who made people feel more than good enough. Bert knew that I needed a friend. He knew that I didn't know how to make friends, as hard as I tried. Bert was my friend in need for a season and a reason.

Kindergarten: School Daze

My first day of kindergarten at Providence Academy was also my first time out of my parents' eyeball control. My first day of school is a day that I will never forget. Looking back on this school launch pad, I can see now that it was clearly a harbinger of the course of my formal education and much of my life to follow. Once my mother dropped me off at the school, I had difficulty mixing with other students. I was lonely and lacked social integration and connection skills, so I preferred to sit in the back of the classroom pouting and crying until my mommy returned after a few hours to pick me up. My kindergarten teacher fussed over me to no avail. The rest of the year was a blur. Somehow I got through it. It was at this time that I met Bert, the bus driver.

As parishioners in St. Joseph's Church, my family was recognized by the powers that be as short on dough. We were offered Christmas charity baskets but my parents wouldn't take anything from the church as charity was for "poor people." The meager earnings of my parents were not spent by my parents on booze and smokes. They were giving me and my two siblings, with one on the way, the best they had but I was realizing more and more that something was missing and that I would have to learn to make my own way.

1953: First Grade

Sister Rita Claire was an angel. She loved and cared for all of her students. When I arrived in her class it was noticeably different for me than so much that had come before. The affection which she extended to me warms my heart to this day. When she died in 2011, I cut her picture out of the obituary column and proudly pasted it into my journal.

Frequently, my mother would come to school to visit with Sister Rita Claire. As I sat in the back of the room, as I was instructed, so that the two of them could powwow, talk about me, I admired how young and beautiful both women were. I calculated then that my mother was only 26 years old. My mother and my first grade teacher got along so well that it made the year fly by really fast for me. I was momentarily content between my school work with a sympathetic and caring teacher and being an assistant bus driver with my friend Bert.

During my first grade year, we'd moved into our new home outside of the WWII project neighborhood. Moving from a WWII project home in 1953 to our second home was a very big deal. The original owners of the home on South Mount Shasta made the purchase of the home a real possibility for my parents by letting them buy the home on contract. It was a nice home, a real step up from the war project home. The folks from whom my parents purchased our new home were wonderful people. They carried the mortgage for my parents the first several years, because my folks couldn't qualify for the loan. My folks lived in that home for nearly 50 years.

Once we settled into our home, my father and I had some family business to tend to right away. Brownie was our family cocker spaniel and my constant companion. One day at the veterinary clinic with our little Brownie on a leash, my father and I received some very bad news. We were told that Brownie was very sick and would experience a painful death in the next few weeks. It was expensive for my parents to call upon a vet at the clinic, and there weren't any funds to have our puppy put to sleep by the vet, so my father loaded Brownie and the two of us up in his 1941 Oldsmobile and we rode off into the forest northeast of Vancouver, Washington.

My father had packed his .22 caliber pistol for the ride out to the forest. I wondered why my father packed a pistol, but in short order I would learn the drill. Once we arrived at our destination, my dad pulled our car over to the side of the forestry road. He took a few items out of the trunk. He immediately pounded a stake in the ground and tethered Brownie to the stake with her doggie leash, and in a few minutes as I watched her sad eyes looking directly into my father's eyes, my dad shot the family pet dead. I cried all the way home and was told that it was a tough thing to do, but with no extra money, what choices did we have? My father did what he needed to do. Tough love.

My mom and dad had big plans for our family in our new home. We were now a family of six: two parents and four boys. Immediately after moving in, I was led to my bedroom at the top of the stairs, with one light bulb hanging from exposed electrical wires. There was no insulation and no heat, and it wasn't until after I left home in 1965 that there was heat installed upstairs where we boys slept.

I really liked having my new bedroom all to myself but it was brrrr … cold in the winter. My other two brothers shared a room down the hall. Age has its privileges.

I was proud of our new house but I was too embarrassed to bring friends over because we weren't good enough, because we couldn't afford insulation or heat in my bedroom, no wall board, just naked studs. My dad worked hard to insulate the upstairs for his boys but by the time the upstairs was well insulated, I already had isolated myself from any school pals. Each and every week, as I went to mass at church, I observed those around me. I couldn't help but notice the new cars in the church's parking lot, who had money, who was wearing the mink stoles, who was wearing the French cuffs and cufflinks, as everyone seemed to be wearing all their material possessions "on their sleeves." I felt uneasy, embarrassed, and uncomfortable because in this house of prayer each and every Sunday, we were reminded that we were a poor family.

After mass one Sunday while Roy Bergeron, the gas station attendant at the local Richfield station was pumping gas at 19 cents a gallon, I was standing up on the hump in the back seat of our 1950 Dodge coupe between the driver and the passenger's seats, listening to my parents chat as they pored through the church's tithing list. I began to ask why my folks were so sad. I soon learned that among the hundreds of families putting money in the weekly church collection basket, our family appeared dead last on the tithing list. Imagine the humiliation at school and at church I experienced. Imagine how devastated my parents were feeling.

Whenever I see lists such as this one published, I think of the damage that this shaming has caused to me and to others at the bottom of a list. I remember the names even now of those who created the list and the people on the top of that list. Many of those other poor parishioners have been shunned their entire lives. I know I was. There were 500-plus families who belonged to St. Joseph's Church parish in the 1950s, and the news traveled fast. I wonder to this day why the pastor of our church would permit such financial numbers to be sprinkled out among the parishioners. This was a life-sculpting moment for me, at age five, and for my parents too I am sure. It served to remind them frequently of how poor they were. Like they needed to be reminded.

To this day, whenever I see or hear of a list ranking people's donations and weekly offerings, I tend not to contribute. Where were these people when I wasn't good enough? I'm not joining the list to show others that I am not at the bottom of the list. Even today, when I go to a school or church fundraising event, when I hear the phrase "and who would be comfortable giving at this level," I'm ready for the door. Sometimes I bolt. Do we think our childhood shapes us?

1954: Second Grade

By the time I started second grade we were firmly ensconced in our new home.

My second grade teacher Miss Mattice was an angel; she was a babe, too. She did all that one could do to help me to get along in her class. She knew that being an angel to me would make her teaching job much easier while giving me much needed attention which I was starved for at the time, something which I didn't fully comprehend. She was a young teacher and I really think her heart was pure. But she truly had her work cut out for her when it came to me.

During the second grade, Miss Mattice was constantly celebrating me as a bright kid. She recognized my strong math skills and often had students from other grades come to our classroom lined-up to compete against me at the blackboard to see who would do the multiplication tables faster than I could. While this experience made me feel good and proud of my math accomplishments, it was a complicated schoolhouse dynamic.

The politics among the teachers about promoting this vagabond schoolboy reverberated up and down the schoolhouse corridors. The losers at the blackboard would often find me on the playground to push me around a bit … pick a fight with me. I was no match on the playground for the bigger guys in the fifth and sixth grades. So I was bullied a bit, which produced daily quarrels and squabbles on the school playground. I had become so good at math that other kids in the school started to hate my guts.

One day returning from recess, a kid whom I had bested earlier in the day at the math blackboard slammed me up against the wall. Oh did I hurt; my face was all bruised up for a long time. I thought, Tom, you are a big roly-poly bully, but it was I who was sporting a black eye. Is this sportsmanship-like conduct? If I had been the bully I would have been sent to the rectory on the well-beaten path which I had already come to know so well. But in this case, Tom was asked to just knock it off.

Why was I so quick in math? My father, a shift worker, wanted me to become someone that he didn't become. He already felt that life had passed him by. My father had only a third grade education. Later on, I learned that he was a lost child – his father was absent. Each day after he returned from work at the paper mill for the first few years of my schooling, my father would have his lunch pail empty except for one important gift for me. At the bottom of his lunch bucket he had left a few pieces of paper with some math problems which he had scribbled for me to complete. Extra work. He was sharing what he could contribute to my education process, so that I could be all that I could be, a smart kid in math.

He worked at the paper mill and did so for more than 40 years in the kraft mill department, the stinkiest department in the mill. The plumes of steam cast a putrid smell that permeated the far reaches of Clark County, Washington, all during my childhood. Before my father came home after his work shift, he needed to shower and leave his clothes at work.

No wonder while growing up I never could proudly say that is where my father worked. The fumes that emanate from the mill to this day remind me of my father's life and how he struggled to make economic ends meet. During his career at the mill, his compensation was barely above minimum pay. In my late teens, when I was on the payroll at the mill, I visited his place of work. The environment where he worked was out of bounds for anyone without a special pass and certainly not a stop along the mill's daily visitor tours for those who wanted to learn how paper is manufactured. Rarely did my father see anyone else on his job except for a cranky foreman who in his working career was the lead worker specializing in management moodiness. His isolation at work afforded him the time to prepare math papers for me and to make items in the millwright shop that we couldn't afford to purchase on his meager earnings. Not until he was near retirement did he ever see a woman in his workplace. His isolation clearly spilled over into my lack of early social development and clearly didn't develop him to climb the union ladder.

My father's lack of education and development set the tone for his frustration with the world. While he complained under his breath that life wasn't fair, he worked his butt off to make ends meet at the cost of considerable lost sleep. He showed us all how to work hard to keep our heads above water, an enduring work ethic imprint.

My father died of lung cancer, but I didn't know that until they did an autopsy on him to determine the cause of his death. My father was so numbed out from all the pain in which he lived, he didn't even know the pain he felt, he died of a poor man's disease, it is suspected, from the toxic chemical fumes and dust permeating the environment in which he worked at the paper mill's kiln department.

In the second grade, I was not only the celebrated student body math whiz kid but I was asked to be the master of ceremonies at the student body assemblies. What an honor to be asked, as I was only in the second grade. I was told by my teacher Miss Mattice that I was very good as a public speaker and was terrific with the microphone. I felt proud to be leading the school assembly for the entire student body. Imagine: there were kids all the way through eighth grade sitting out in the audience.

Sad, but true, I was nearly 50 years of age when I was asked to speak from the podium again. My first experience at the podium was at a Rotary Club meeting at the Hotel Regina, Paris, France. I truly had been benched and squelched during my formative years. I recognized that the teachers frequently discussed my schoolyard behavior. I had some teachers who recognized my abilities and others who felt that I was not a good kid. I continued to operate under the stigma of being a bad boy. My parents may have known what was going on concerning how I was being treated or what my behavior was in school. My parents were not good enough in their own minds to call on the school leadership to discuss my deportment issues.

The second grade ushered in a new beginning of many years and tears of humiliation in school. Each school quarter the parish priest, Father Thomas J. Posh, would come into the classroom, take his position at our teacher's desk, front and center, the power spot, and call out our names one at a time in alphabetical order. As each of our names was called we approached the front of the classroom. Father then publicly commented individually on our academic grades by subject, our deportment status, and our attendance record. I dreaded being called to the front of the room. I knew that I was going to be scolded. The public humiliation I received labeled me as a poor student and reinforced the public image that I was a bad boy. Squelched!

I was aware that I had a lot of potential talent but who would come to my rescue? I was great in math and could get up to speak on my feet.

Without financial resources and self-confidence, my parents were so busy making ends meet that I had to fight my own battles. If you were a moneyed family in this parish, you had a voice with privileges. Certainly, those financially well-off families had done a better job of teaching their children exemplary behavior patterns. They were better socially integrated and socially developed. However, if the true measure of people is exhibited in their compassion and kindness toward others, it didn't come through with these rich kids.

To be a member of St. Joseph's Church in good standing was all about who has what and in whose home Father Posh would be dining this weekend. What else is new? A multi-generational behavior pattern class-struggle was already in the making.

On the other hand, while I was embarrassed many times during report card reviews, I am grateful and proud that Father Posh taught me the value of a good firm handshake and a very readable signature. In my mind, as a result of his publicly administered criticism, he fell short in his ability to be a true leader and source of inspiration.

Frequently, many years later, I am complimented on my firm handshake and my very readable signature, two things that say so much about a person.

I learned from Father Posh but he was someone who gave so much but also lacked so much.

The old adage of public praise and private criticism was not his skill set. Does my directness today in my mannerisms come from him, or from my being benched, or from making up for what my folks were unable to do, which is stick up for one's self? If my parents had been well-educated, well-off, and big contributors to the school, I know that I would have been treated with kindness at church and at school. Money talks!

1955: Third Grade

I survived the third grade uneventfully. This year was a blur.

Mrs. Berg had a reputation for being a tough cookie. She was a rigid teacher with no time for bullshit. Her rules of engagement were well etched on her visage. Talk about a report card. I minded my "p's and q's." I slid safely into the next grade. I toed the mark. Bottom line, it was her way or the highway.

During this school year, I remember more about looking for a paper route to make some money than paying any attention to school work.

On Sunday afternoons, my dad was frequently at the paper mill working swing-shift. While Dad was at work my mom needed a little break, so we'd all pile into the family auto and go to visit my mother's parents. We kids always enjoyed going to the grandparents' home. My mother got the relief she was looking for by sharing kid care duties with her parents.

It was always interesting to visit with my grandparents, who lived around the corner from Peninsula Park in Portland, Oregon. My grandmother always had much to say. However, one day I remember her, during an advertising break on the popular *Ed Sullivan Show*, telling me that I would be a very good attorney. However, in the next breath she told my mother, "Don't encourage him to go to law school—look at that mouth on him!" Dissed again.

I really liked my grandmother, but I wondered why she would say such a thing. To this day, I wish I had become an attorney; I know well that I would have been a good one. Only later did I realize that her comment served to bench me for some time. I also learned later that my grandmother was not a supporter of strong and accomplished men. In addition, she detested smoking and ridiculed others for it but after her death, it was announced that she was a closet smoker.

My grandmother passed away over the Thanksgiving holiday weekend in 1971. To this day during Thanksgiving weekends, I am reminded of her passing and happy to know that she is resting in a more peaceful place.

During this time I was beginning to feel the pain of being put down, shunned, and pigeonholed by my family because I wasn't good enough. Is this domestic violence? I think so. I began to recognize increasingly in the third grade that our family didn't have enough money to go shopping like my classmates' families. Despite being the oldest son, I was wearing hand-me-downs. Yes, I was sporting someone's faded salt and pepper cords. It was obvious that I wasn't wearing new duds when the school year began.

I was constantly being scolded by my parents and being told that I was a bad boy. My feelings were numbed and that is why I didn't cry; I didn't know how to cry. I was taught that crying was reserved for funerals. I was experiencing my own childhood being hijacked. I was unaware that I was being taught to be a tough guy. In time this script played out as I continued to act out. I was hooked up to a chemo drip of toxic shame!

My folks had grown a garden at our new home and the produce consisted of red and green tomatoes with heads of lettuce. My lunch bucket was typically packed with tomato and lettuce sandwiches, which were always soggy by lunch time. My schoolmates were always comparing what they had in their sandwiches at school. I was so embarrassed to share with others what I was eating that I never sat with anyone at lunch. I didn't have an apple or an orange or any candy bars, but most kids had goodies to barter. There was nothing of value in my lunchbox. I was alone on the end of the lunch bench.

1956: Fourth Grade

I wasn't cracking the school books but Mrs. Wilma Kuepfer, my fourth grade teacher, was a patron saint in my book.

Mrs. Kuepfer was a nice elderly lady as I recall. I liked her from the get-go. I went through this grade unscathed. She was best friends with my mom and they were both members of St. Benedict's Circle, a church volunteer group. Mrs. Kuepfer was so nice to me that I managed to make it through the year. Her good treatment of me was like a tonic.

In this school year I learned that I had a future in the newspaper business, which held my attention beyond school or school work. I was into scouting, selling and delivering newspapers, chasing girls, riding my bike, and helping my father remodel our home for our ever-expanding Catholic family.

This was the year of many firsts for me. I was begging for a job selling newspapers from the local circulation manager, cigar-chomping Bill W., who drove a red land-yacht convertible. He was the manifestation of someone *nouveau riche*. He had a lock on who in his circulation district was to be a newspaper boy delivering the only newspaper in town, the *Vancouver*

Columbian. Big shot Bill didn't dig my style too much so I was left selling for an on-strike Portland-based newspaper called the *Oregon Journal.*

Since Bill wouldn't hire me with my rock 'n' roll attitude at ten years of age, I signed on with the *Oregon Journal.* Imagine, I was selling the *Journal,* which was an "on strike" newspaper, in mill town Vancouver, a totally rough and tough blue-collar community

In short order I became the *Journal's* top flight newspaper sales agent. Determination and focus was my stairway to the top. With dough flow, cash in my pocket, school was far down on the list of my priorities but I was the best-dressed kid in the school house. Bill may have labeled me a bad boy but I looked spiffy. Elvis would have been proud of me in my white bucks.

Finally, we were graced with Father Posh's presence as a dinner guest at our home. I'll never forget this early afternoon dinner. Prior to Father coming to our home for dinner, we were indoctrinated by our parents on the expectations concerning our behavior. I was put on notice, I was the oldest, and I was held accountable and responsible for my brothers' behavior. Why did we rate having dinner with Father at our home? I could do the math. I thought something was cooking. We hadn't won the lottery nor had my father received a huge raise from the boss he despised at the mill. Later, I learned that my father was an accomplished, non-licensed electrician and plumber, trades he had learned from his father.

My father, it turns out, was donating his time to help with repairs at the church. Father Posh needed something from our family. Time is money. This special dinner was an evening that I'll never forget. We were short a dining chair. Where was I to sit? I was told to go to the bathroom and to bring the clothes hamper to the table and to use it as my seat around the table. Yes, there were dirty clothes in the hamper. Oh my God! Thankfully we didn't have to air our dirty linen in front of Father Posh.

Della Olson moved into the neighborhood. From her first day living next door to us, this bold, brazen, and over-the-top lady began her daily routine. Della was always coming to our home with a pot of fresh-brewed coffee in hand, decked out in a muumuu. She could be heard making her entry at our back door always yelling "Yoo-hoo, yoo-hoo."

My brothers and I loved Della; she frequently brought along cinnamon rolls that she baked. She always had so much gossip to share with Mom that we kids got a break from our mother's close order drill. Della had no children, so she became the aunt we loved until we discovered girls. Then she got too nosey.

It is at about this time that my dad started moonlighting by picking up some extra bucks mowing lawns for some rich folks who lived a mile or two down the street from us. These folks lived on the bluff overlooking the river and they enjoyed a magnificent view of Portland's city lights. I like it that my dad was working hard to make some money. Christmas was coming; we all wanted to have a nice Christmas, which meant lots of presents for us kids under the tree.

My dad doing this yard work was difficult for me because the lawns that my father mowed and the flower beds that needed weeding meant that my father was literally on his knees working for the parents of my grade school classmates. I found this humiliating because I would constantly be reminded by my schoolmates that they had seen my dad. I knew where they saw my dad. I knew that they did not see him in the paper mill since his department was off limits to anyone who was not employed in that dangerous department. So, my classmates were telling me that my dad was working in their yards and I got it about why they were telling me.

1957: Fifth Grade

In the fifth grade, I was on the street selling newspapers. I wasn't able to get a job delivering newspapers for the *Vancouver Columbian* because I was told that I wasn't old enough. I continued to sell newspapers for the *Oregon Journal*, Route 368. I was proud. It was not a very big route. There were not many Vancouverites at the time who were interested in the Portland published newspapers in my local mill town. My parents were nonplussed with me acquiring a paper route for a newspaper that soon went on strike, with scab workers publishing the newspaper.

My father was a staunch union man even though he never wielded any union power. Against great odds, I built up this route to generate more newspaper sales. I became so enamored with this challenge that my route manager took a real liking to me. She taught me how to sell. And sell newspapers I did. Irene Rupe, my manager, was a beautiful lady.

Now this is the year that made life worth living. In my fifth year of grade school, Sister Francesca was the teacher who became my archangel. I could do no wrong in her eyes. On many an occasion this teacher went to bat for me. She took a lot of flak for being not only my teacher but my best buddy, mentor, and advocate. Yes, I was teacher's pet. I had love! In fact, I think that I fell in love with her. She had all the criteria. She was nice, smart, good looking, and gave me unconditional love. My grades in her class were not anything to write home about but they were better than I had received from any other teacher. Frequently, she had to defend herself for being so fond of me, and our fondness was mutual.

Rain or shine throughout this school year, I would ride each Saturday morning to the schoolhouse to work side by side with Sister Francesca just the two of us, helping her prepare for the following week's class curriculum. I felt good and it was so wonderful to be around this lady.

Sister Francesca was an angel; she loved me. She provided me with a respite from all the hell that was going on around me. I didn't know it at the time but she really did like me and was worried about me, and she was doing the Lord's work.

When Sister Superior, the mother superior, and Father Posh, the parish priest, found out that Sister Francesca really was fond of me, we were immediately separated. We were split up. My world came crashing down. I had been looking for some love and acceptance, and I was getting some. Soon I was again lonely. No way! I was needy but what is one to do? I had someone whom I could count on ... for a while. How awkward and sad for me.

Again, I was abandoned, I was culled out. I was not good enough. During this school year I learned from a fellow patrol boy named Dennis Knable all about the birds and the bees. Dennis was holding out the flag to stop the traffic as I was told to get off my bike and to walk it across the crosswalk and to listen. "Terry, have you ever heard of sex and masturbation?" I thought what in the hell is going on here? I'm walking across the street in the crosswalk at the corner of MacArthur and SE Andersen Rd., on my way to St. Joseph's Grade School. Life began to change. I've never forgotten Dennis Knable and every time I drive through that intersection I have memories of the sexual enlightenment he provided to me.

In the fifth grade I was fully employed after school as a newspaper boy rain or shine. I also found a few extra lawn jobs to bring in a few more dollars to support myself and take the pressure off my parents a little.

Prior to becoming an altar boy, which was expected of all sixth, seventh, and eighth grade boys, I had to learn rote phrases in Latin. It was difficult to learn the Latin responses but with private coaching by the parish priest, Father Posh, I became an altar boy.

This was also the year that I would "try out" for a little league team. I made it; I was put on a minor league team called TCP. The coach's name was Richard Votive. His son Joe was on my team, and since his father was the coach, Joe always played first base. Mr. Votive took me on his team because of a sense of duty to his fellow church parishioners, my parents. While I was one of the team members, I was a full-time bench warmer. I played three innings all season. I was proud to be on the team but I knew that as co-coordinated as I was, I was again seen as the bad boy. Benched.

When my father spoke to the coach to ask why I wasn't playing, he was told that I needed glasses. Maybe that was the case but why didn't the coach say something up front as the season began rather than let the season play out? My father wasn't strong enough to share a piece of his mind with Mr. Votive.

The following year my father had an answer to Mr. Votive's put down. In 1957, my father founded T-Ball as his way of getting every kid into the game.

School was an interruption in my work life, a life that was active for me at ten and eleven years of age. I was delivering newspapers, mowing lawns and pulling weeds for the neighbors, becoming an altar boy, learning from Dennis Knable, my friend, about sex, in love with my teacher, flirting with classmate Rhonda Cole, and learning how to be a bench warmer. Della was delivering cinnamon rolls. I was on a roll. But I was a lonely bad boy, at work, at school, at home, and at play. Coincidentally at the same time that the patrol boy began to educate me about sex, I was going to learn some more from my father.

My parents decided that it was time to enlarge our home, which meant a lot to them and to all of us kids. My dad soon figured out after the city issued us a remodeling permit on our home that we didn't have the money to have our home professionally rebuilt. My father was the architect, the carpenter, the plumber, and the electrician. I overheard most of the discussions about the cost for each and every item to remodel our home. The one project that had a huge impact on me was the first decision my father made about remodeling. Dad told me that we needed to go to the local lumber yard to buy a couple of shovels.

"Why?" I asked.

"Terry, you are going to help me dig out the new basement."

I was told that to save money we would have to dig the basement by hand. I thought I already had enough other jobs to do. My paper route on my Schwinn bicycle was my flight to freedom. No, again my wings were clipped.

This physical digging out of the basement "project" went on for more than two years. And I am still emotionally digging out from this experience. It became my dad's obsession, and mine as well, because I was so embarrassed that once again, I couldn't play with my school buddies. I had to work because we didn't have any money to hire someone with the machinery to dig the basement for us.

It wasn't like this project was being done behind the house out of sight of the neighbors and my classmates. We were digging a basement in the front yard for all the world to see and to supervise. In 1957 … it was from this dirt pile that I saw Sputnik fly over.

The remodel project went on for more than 10 years, and wasn't completed until after I was married in 1970. The finishing touches were put on the house days before my parent's 25th wedding anniversary, which was celebrated at their home in 1971. The one and only time I ever saw my father tipsy was at this party, after several goblets of champagne. Good for him, he earned it!

My father said, "Son, keep your head down, keep digging, and today you are going to learn about the birds and the bees." I had discovered Elvis Presley shaking his hips and chasing chicks so I was curious, and the facts of life came to me.

I learned that my buddy Dennis was right and that I no longer needed to shun him. I was now motivated to meet with Irene Rupe, my newspaper route boss, with the sexy legs, at every opportunity. I enjoyed watching her jumping in and out of the car. I never had the courage to go after her. She was three times older than I was but I hit sales goals off the charts. No wonder. She inspired me. She taught me how to sell. She cared for me. Now that I couldn't spend time with Sister Francesca, I had a new love.

Later as a result of Mrs. Rupe's sales training, I did so well selling newspapers in 1959 that I won a sales contest and was eventually on a Western Airlines flight to Mexico City for one week. I was making more money than my parents.

Later, I was to learn that Bill W. had "the hots" for Irene Rupe. He was jealous of me. It so happens that we all met at the same intersection on Lieser Road to pick up our papers for delivery—either from the local *Vancouver Columbian*, or the on strike newspaper, the *Oregon Journal* from across the river in Portland.

One day when I was out with Mrs. Rupe she asked me if I knew of anyone who might like some extra work. I inquired what kind of work that might be. Mrs. Rupe went on to tell me that she was looking for a district driver, someone with a car, to pick up newspapers from the central distribution point and then redistribute them to all the other newspaper boys in her district, essentially all of east Vancouver.

My parents welcomed the opportunity to make some money to support our growing family. Our 1953 Mercury station wagon was turned into a family work horse. After a few months, our family car was now a delivery truck and it smelled like a printing press with black ink everywhere, just like your hands look after reading a fresh daily newspaper. The extra money helped out the family but driving around town, I felt like a clown. No pride.

As I was growing up, I was constantly working out of need. The family's economic situation was difficult. I was delivering three newspaper routes. I had two newspaper routes with the *Journal* and finally I was able to get Bill W. to give me at least one Vancouver newspaper route.

It was at about this time that I started combing the classified ads for berry picking and bean picking jobs. Each summer, many school kids, me included, saw the need to make a little extra cash. Like me, many of us enjoyed the berry fields and bean picking as a way to get out in the fields to meet some girls as well as make some money. I loved it. I preferred working in the bean fields as the crops grow higher and it was easier to hide from the farm owners who were always spying on their school kid helpers. Sue Lindeman and I had a thing going and to this day, whenever I drive by a bean field I think of her and wonder what she might be doing today. I was always infatuated with her, she was cute as a button, but I could tell that her big sister was the experienced one but I never had the courage to go for it.

My career in the berry fields with my berry friends didn't last too many seasons. Once again my rock 'n' roll attitude was my constant companion and it got me into trouble. If I couldn't pick beans with the Lindeman sisters, I was not a very happy camper. I really liked the Alexander sisters in the berry fields but except for a little necking with Rickie Alexander I wasn't too excited about the berry fields. No place to hide.

In addition to all the newspaper sales and delivery, and a little crop harvesting, I was pulling weeds and mowing the lawn for the neighbors, Thad and Jean Icebox.

I did whatever it took to support myself, and I was helping my parents by taking an economic load off of them. I was basically begging to work to have some money to buy clothing, food, and a right to be validated. I was looking to be accepted. Earning was my yearning, so I could feel like I was somebody!

The house was always under construction, and the never-ending digging out of the basement when I went home meant I could never just sit around. If my dad was at home, it meant work.

1n 1957, my father received word that his father died in Mt. Morris, Illinois, of a heart attack. My father wasn't going to go to his father's funeral. He had no extra money. When the news spread around the neighborhood, Tom and Pauline Hewitt from across the street came over and consoled my father, the only day that I ever saw my father cry. The Hewitts gave my dad two twenty-dollar bills. At the time this was so much money that my mother sewed the two bills into his t-shirt so that he wouldn't lose the money sleeping on the train for three days and nights. A few years earlier forty dollars was more than one week's take-home pay for my father. This experience really drove home the point that we were economically challenged.

My dad and mother wanted so much to have a beautiful home filled with loving kids and then they thought everything would be so wonderful. They would be proud. They were Catholics. My father was a convert to Catholicism and my mother lived the religion from the time she was born. Later, I was to learn that a condition of their marriage was that my father "had to" become a Catholic. He did, and he became a strict Catholic.

The Catholic Church didn't believe in birth control, and they still don't. It was soon after my father gave me the story of the birds and the bees that I discovered my mother's handiwork—I found hand-stitched sexy underwear that she had sewn. I was sure that they were having sex. For some odd reason no kid ever thinks their parents have sex. That is what they were doing when I was put to work warming my dad's jockeys on the old stove. Things were adding up.

Around the house whatever my mother wanted, my father did. I am sure he got his rewards for being so obedient.

As I look back, I wonder whether my parents consciously or unconsciously knew they had built themselves a prison through their desire to be good Catholics and procreate and have a big, wonderful home to house everyone. As the oldest it was incumbent on me to go to work. I felt pressure to add to the family larder. Growing up, I never saw a book or a magazine around the house. There was a dictionary, but on the infrequent occasions when there was need to look up a word, it was a chore to find it.

1958: Sixth Grade

After a wonderful year with my fifth grade teacher, my sixth grade year was a study in contrast. Sister Immaculata, an older nun, was a battle-ax … a mean cookie. She knew it. She was proud of it. As I've grown older

I realize there are reasons to this day for her behavior that I do not completely understand, but it represents why the play *Late Night Catechism* continues to be so popular. In my fifth grade year, a troublemaker, a bad boy like me, had his work cut out for him, as I soon learned.

This was a long year at good old St. Joseph's. Father Posh had met his match too. Sister Immaculata ran her class her way and took no heat from anyone. I was constantly in the doghouse. I wore a path during this school year from her class room to the rectory office. When Sister Immaculata grew tired of my Elvis Presley attitude she marched me off to see Father Posh at the rectory for the rest of the day. "He is a bad boy, so Father, you take care of him. He is your problem."

Thank God I had a newspaper route cause it was something to do. I would deliver papers after school and then I would go knocking door to door to sell new subscriptions. I enjoyed signing up new customers. I increased my route size, I was handsomely rewarded by the newspaper with trips up and down the west coast to Seattle, to Bremerton, and to Disneyland. I was being honored for being a good boy and for making newspaper sales.

In the sixth grade, I was all about Elvis Presley and more. Elvis had a girlfriend, Ann-Margret, and I needed one, too. My hormones were already working overtime. I had a girlfriend and her name was Rhonda. She was beautiful, a real cutie. I chased her the entire year and was infatuated with her so much so that I would buy her jewelry from my newspaper earnings. When I look back over the years, I wonder what happened to my old flame. I miss passing those love notes in class. On occasion Sister Immaculata would discover what I was up to and stand me in the corner.

This was also the year that all good little Catholic boys became altar boys. In those days, we had to learn our altar boy responses in Latin. I had difficulty learning my lines but Father Posh tutored me, I became an altar boy. I was so proud to be an altar boy and to feel so much closer to God. Whenever I had the opportunity I would taste the wine in the sacristy. Oh it was yummy!

Becoming an altar boy was solely Father Posh's decision, and much to my sixth grade teacher's chagrin, she didn't have a vote on the decision.

My teacher was into punishing me, not celebrating me, particularly in the celebration at mass.

Father had an agenda; he had plans for me to become a priest. He recognized my talents and overlooked my deportment unless the teachers voiced their dismay, which put him on the spot. I was the ongoing football being kicked from goal to goal.

I had many intersections with scouting activities through junior high school, but I had mixed reaction to my scouting experiences. My young mind at the time could clearly see that the dads who had the money and the power were the members of the "old boys" network that ran scouting. I didn't fit in, nor did my family. I wanted to belong but always I was not quite good enough. It didn't take rocket science to figure out who was in the in-crowd and who wasn't.

One year, I wanted so badly to go to Camp Meriwether for Boy Scouts, along the Oregon coast. However, to attend camp I needed to have a Boy Scout uniform. I didn't have a uniform, so my parents borrowed a uniform shirt from a family friend.

Bottom-line, at my insistence, I went to camp, and while at camp attempting to earn a lifesaving merit badge, I lost the shirt after I inflated it, as we were instructed to do, to serve as a flotation device. I made a mistake and the shirt went straight to the bottom of the lake. The Boy Scout shirt went so deep in the lake I was unable to recover it. I spent the rest of the week as the only scout of a few hundred scouts out of uniform. Needless to say my parents paid the family for the lost shirt, and my newspaper earnings were garnished for a couple of months. My scouting career was short-lived. Scouting did not feel like a place of welcome for a poor kid. To this day, when I hear of others who made the rank of Eagle Scout being congratulated, I am reminded of my attempt to belong. Again, not good enough, I was benched once more.

I was too much of a lightweight to play football. But baseball I could play. However, for some reason, I couldn't play with consistency. I was a good pitcher on the mound and if left unshackled I could strike out nearly everyone in every game. Didn't happen. Once I got rattled by the opposing team, which happened frequently, the wheels would come off and I would not be able to continue as a pitcher in the game. I was an extraordinarily good pitcher, but I was not built to be laughed at. My self-confidence was so far down in the dumps that I didn't have the resiliency to let the negative comments and vibes roll off my back. Again, I was benched.

This same scenario played out for me in Little League. As mentioned earlier, I had made the minor league team TCP of Columbia Little League Baseball in the McLoughlin Heights neighborhood of east Vancouver. The coach, Richard Votive, did his best but even then I could tell he played his favorite players.

My father was frustrated watching me not playing in the league designed for kids, and he was saddened to see me warming the bench. I was proud; I was a member of the team. I felt badly that I did not play more but I was a team member.

To avoid bench warming for my younger brother, my father devised a new concept inspired by the bench warmers in Little League. He was one of the pioneers of T-ball. He never took credit for his invention, nor did he even know how to find a patent for his eleemosynary invention. (In addition, apparently other men in various parts of the country also developed the T-ball concept during the mid-1950s.) He wasn't interested in making money, only in looking out for the little guys and those other kids like me who were having a hard time earning some playing time on field as a member on a team. My father wanted us all to have what he never received in life, a break. He could see history repeating itself.

T-ball afforded every kid the opportunity to play baseball by first teeing up the ball, hitting it, and running like hell to first base. From my father's perspective every kid should have an opportunity to play and not spend the season warming a bench. It wasn't until years later that I recognized that my father had a big heart for the down-and-out kids who were at a disadvantage. He played to his level. It wasn't good enough but he did the best he could. T-ball was a huge attempt by my father to get me and his boys, along with all the other kids, off the bench and on to the playing field of life.

The sixth grade was the year that boys discovered girls and the girls discovered the boys. Why did we have to take dance lessons in this school grade from this teacher, Sister Immaculata? This battle-ax was anything other than a dance instructor. She was a "dance Nazi," as we often referred to her. How were we to learn how to dance from a gal who clearly didn't like boys, particularly those like me trying to have a good time? She wasn't exactly thrilled about my Elvis Presley haircut … and white bucks … or dancing too close with the girls, which was then taboo … frequently the twelve-inch ruler didn't find the space required between my dance partner and myself, and I was asked to sit on the bench.

A top ten tune, "Wake Up Little Susie," by the Everly Brothers was *verboten* for Catholic kids to listen to as was watching Elvis thrust his sexy pelvis. In my 40's, I took private dancing lessons to regain my dancing feet after having been humiliated by this nun and others. Finally, off the bench and onto the dance floor, where I learned to dance, as the saying goes, like nobody is watching.

Sister Immaculata was into punishing me on a daily basis. Mike Mulligan turned me in for saying "dog" backwards on the playground so I was kicked off the recess ball field. Bad boy. When Bob Young, a bully, beat me up, my dad beat me up. I wasn't even safe at home.

My sixth grade teacher was ruthless and she let you know who was boss. I challenged her and she kind of liked it because I was a match for her. But whenever I would say a naughty word in class after one of my fellow classmates turned me in for my behavior at recess, I was called to the front of the room and the inside of my hands were slapped with the 12-inch ruler. This public humiliation continued to isolate me from my classmates. I cussed and threw a fit so that I would be sent on a trip down the path to the rectory because Father Thomas Posh would look after me, protect me.

That year Grandma Beard, my father's mother, traveled from Chicago to Portland on the Union Pacific Railroad; it took her three days but she made it. We boys loved her. She was non-Catholic, agnostic, and laughed all the time at nothing and everything. I heard the words "shit" and "fuck" so many times that I thought I was living in a new world. She wanted to talk about sex??? Needless to say, my Catholic mother wasn't too happy with her, and my father was punished. Mother was distancing herself from him. No longer was my father allowed to slap my mother's cute little butt.

I didn't learn until later that these little pats were a precursor to baby making. Remember the oil stove?

The priest asked my parents if we wanted a food basket at Christmas. Ouch! Who wants someone else's recycled holiday fruitcake?

1959: Seventh Grade

Sister Andrea was a cool teacher. Tall and athletic with an engaging smile, she and I hit it off famously. I would not call her an angel but she ranked right up there, caring for me as she did for my fellow classmates. I tried to become her pet but she didn't quite let me make the cut like Sister Francesca but Sister Andrea, now she was a good sport. She graded me and others fairly and I knew where I stood with her.

Sr. Andrea was a tall, geeky person with a wonderful demeanor who liked my spunk and feistiness because she was just like me, or at least so I thought.

1960: Eighth Grade: Starting to Rock 'n' Roll

Finally, my parents had a daughter. Now we had a Terrill, Darrell, and Errol, Gary and Jeff, and the youngest one was a daughter named Cheryl. My mother always wanted a little girl. The stillborns and those of us who lived waited a long time for her to give birth to her dream … a baby girl. Her mother, my grandmother, would always say to my mother, "Elaine, you should have daughters because they will be more loyal to you than the boys. Once the boys are married they will be gone." If this wasn't a set-up, I didn't know what was. But it was real. Words do have impact. We boys were benched again.

Sister Superior was the school principal; she was a cool eighth grade teacher, bright, happy and quick. She was rules and order but we got along famously because she had great people skills … and knew how to handle me so I could graduate from the eighth grade, as she was potentially the roadblock to my diploma. I was so busy selling newspapers that school didn't mean much to me other than to go through the motions to get the passing grades and be on my way to St. Edwards Seminary, near Seattle, a three-hour drive north of Vancouver.

It was tradition at my grade school that in the last week of the school year before graduation ceremonies there was a graduating class "sneak day … a class skip day." This was a day that I'll never forget. I was still sporting my rock 'n' roll attitude, so the teachers decided that I should not be invited along with my classmates on this all-important sneak day. I was told, "Terry, you'll report to the parish rectory." While my fellow students boarded the bus to a fun park, I accompanied our parish pastor Father Posh to a funeral in Woodland, Washington, to assist him as an altar boy. Oh, I felt saintly. There were a couple of people from the funeral home at the graveside service, plus Father and myself. I thought, this man over whose grave we were praying was lonely too. Where was everybody, his family and friends? Some sneak day.

In a few months, I was on my way to the seminary to become a priest. Honestly, I felt like one day I might become ultimately a canonized saint. I was sold on going to the seminary. Maybe I would get some recognition, finally. As philosopher Nietzsche once said, "What doesn't kill me makes me stronger."

1960: January: Mexico City

On a cold winter night in January 1960, as I departed on a Western Airlines propeller airplane to LAX, first stop on my way to Mexico City, the wheels went up and I experienced my first taste of freedom. It was a conscious thought … "freedom." This was my first time to travel on an airplane. I knew it was my flight to freedom for one whole week *sans* parents. My parents had never been on an airplane. It was tough for them to see me go, it was in their eyes, and they knew full well that when I returned I would have seen a slice of the world that they had never seen or would ever see. I was on my way to making my own decisions without being told what, where, and how to do something. Earning money was my first eagerly sought goal so that I could work my way out of wearing "hand me down" school clothes and borrowed Boy Scout uniforms. Wearing worn-out clothes from my classmates badly bruised my child ego. I wasn't good enough to be with others. However, in Mexico City, I was free to begin to create my own worldview. I found my self-efficacy, I became "The little engine that could."

Through my determined and focused newspaper selling efforts, I succeeded in climbing and clawing my way out of the poorhouse. In 1959, as a 12-year-old, I had surpassed all sales goals set by the *Oregon Journal* newspaper by selling new subscriptions, by knocking on doors day and night. No time for school homework. As a result of my success, the newspaper rewarded me with additional money and a free trip, the all-expenses-paid trip to Mexico City. I knew that by accomplishing the goal of being the top-selling newspaper boy, I would be taking my first flight to freedom, with dough in my pocket. I was no longer poor and ashamed. Imagine, more than $300 in my pocket at 12 years of age, and an all-expense paid international trip! I was on my way.

Horatio Alger lives!!

As I arrived at the Continental Hilton, in the heart of Mexico City, I was in awe. My chaperone assigned me to my own room with a few other top-selling newspaper boys in their own rooms down the hall. As I pulled back the blackout drapes, I observed outside, across the hotel's courtyard, people living in abject poverty. I couldn't keep myself from staring and wondering if my hometown plight might not be as bad as I had thought back in SmallVille, USA.

As I was scoping out my new hotel room digs, I continued to ponder in amazement the contrast between the wealth staying in the hotel, me included this week, and the folks outside living between the buildings in makeshift shanties. In the nightstand in my hotel room, I had a choice to make. There was a bible and an autobiography by Conrad Hilton. To this day, I think of Conrad Hilton and his success story when I glance out my office window in Portland at the hotel bearing his name.

This first flight gave birth to more flights, each flight was a flight to freedom, where I could go and explore, *sans* parents, *sans* relatives, nobody telling me what to do, and what to be, which allowed me to create a life my way.

1960: Poisonous—Pedagogy—Paradoxes

Going back in time, one never forgets those moments as a kid growing up that have been life sculpting. To this day, each and every morning as I get dressed, in my walk-in closet, I notice stored on one of the shelves a set of boxing gloves that now are over 50 years old, a collector's item.

As a kid growing up, there wasn't any extra money to go around, but steeped in Catholic tradition, we celebrated holidays. My folks may have struggled to make ends meet but when it came to Christmas everything was "perfect." They would charge up their purchases for the holidays and take the next twelve months to pay off the accumulated balance and begin anew for the next year, an annual tradition, a repetitious cycle.

The holiday season began for us right after the Thanksgiving weekend. To prepare for Christmas, my mother and father would spend days rearranging the living room furniture to make room for the huge Christmas tree freshly cut during a predictably chaotic family outing in the forest. As a group with the best of intentions to be the perfect family, we pitched in to decorate the tree with lights and sundry ornaments, arguing with each other over where each little Christmas doodad would be placed on the tree. After the ritualized evening of decorating the tree as a family, my mother took over.

My mother would, with great pains, pull out of the boxes of icicles (tinsel) one agonizing icicle strand at a time. After many days of my mother's special and dedicated touch, the tree was sculpted and Christmas cards ready, picture perfect, for all the family and relatives to ogle and to comment on about how beautiful the tree looked. As the compliments and comments poured in, my mother would light up like the Christmas tree with pride.

My dad grew up in a little town west of Chicago, in a farm community, Mt. Morris, Illinois. My father never missed an opportunity to tell us about his background. Among the many childhood stories that he'd share, there is one which I remember most. As a kid, his family did not have indoor plumbing but they did have an outhouse. With little money to go around, there was a shortage of money for toilet paper, so they made good by using Sears & Roebuck and Montgomery Ward merchandise catalogs.

It is ironic that years later, my father and mother were now using those same company catalogs to shop for their children's Christmas gifts. This one holiday season, I'll never forget. On my twelfth birthday in 1959, as I reached over to kiss my dad on the cheek to thank him for a little birthday gift, he slapped me and told me I was too old to behave in such a manner. A little later in that same year, I was to receive along with my brothers a Christmas gift that would teach us how to make our way in the world, a set of boxing gloves out of the Sears catalog.

These premium top-of-the-line boxing gloves saw lots of fighting action. Christmas tree or no tree in the living room, our home was transformed into an athletic arena. Today, I can still see this beautiful celebratory picture-perfect tree all decked out and across the room was a cardboard fireplace that I had assembled using colored light bulbs in a stack of logs to give the room the ambiance of a magical Christmas. Our home was complete with a white picket fence. With the drapes wide open, the center of our living room, which was now our boxing ring, provided front-row seats for the passersby.

After the holidays, the boxing gloves continued to see daily use. In fact, one of my brothers got so accomplished with his boxing skills that he would take on my father for a fight after family dinners. In one heated scuffle, my brother shook up my dad so bad that my father went outside to the wood pile. There was no shortage of wood as the house was always in a state of being remodeled. My father returned from the scrap pile with a hefty 4x4. My brother now was on the short end of the stick. My mother and the whole family were yelling and screaming so loudly that I was surprised that the neighbors didn't appear at our door.

Everyone was scared and to this day, I have only a few souvenirs from my youth. A fifth grade photo of me modeled after Elvis Presley, a few of my father's carpentry tools, and yup, the family's famous boxing gloves. I was taught, "Might makes right" and when angry, strike out with your fists!!

1961: St. Edward's Seminary: One Step Closer to Heaven

In the '50s, it was commonplace for the oldest son of Catholic parents to become a priest. So having declared that I was going to the seminary, I was given a little slack in my final year at St. Joseph's. After all, I was headed for the holy land. I was now somebody very important. My parents were tickled. I was pleasing the parish priest, and thereby ingratiating myself with Mom and Dad. I thought by going to the priesthood, I would escape the rigors of home. Maybe by going to the seminary, I would elevate my parents' standing in the church and in the community. Family validation.

Off to St. Edward's Seminary in Kenmore, Washington, I went. This was my first stop on my path to becoming a Catholic priest. Who knows, maybe one day a cardinal and then the pope? There has never been an American pope. My one shot at greatness. The seminary was on a beautiful piece of expensive real estate high on the hills east of Seattle overlooking a beautiful lake.

Now it didn't take me long to figure out this new home away from home, a boarding school environment. This is what I had signed up for to become an ordained priest. Within a couple of weeks, I knew this wasn't the place for me. Only nine more long months to go.

First off, I learned that if you were from a well-known Catholic family in Seattle, wealthy, with great academic standing and athletic prowess, the seminary was your place. However, my folks still had no money; I didn't have great grades and was physically competitive but not emotionally built out for competitive sports. Yes, I got some exercise but never any recognition. Again, I was warming the bench on and off the field. I had retired from the newspaper business, at least temporarily. My study habits were not the best. They never had been. I was again on the bottom of the totem pole.

Looking back over the years, I knew more than I thought I did and wanted to know about the inner workings of the priesthood. I was never the victim of pedophiliac activities but I knew that there was something in the air. I picked up the vibes and the smoke signals. I was too temperamental for anyone to approach me, for they feared that I might talk. I remained vigilant for I had reasons to be. Many years later, we all learned what I'd already known.

Did I escape? Did I go to the seminary because I wanted to be a priest or was it an easy excuse to get out of the house? As it turns out, it was as psychoanalyst Erich Fromm says, an "escape from freedom." My paper routes were my freedom. My Elvis Presley operating style didn't please the priests, nor did it necessarily turn them on.

My dad was the only one to cut my hair until I left for seminary, in the ninth grade. My dad with all his practice cutting his sons' hair had become a very good barber. I had high expectations of other barbers. At the seminary, I was told who was to cut my hair and when. If you were out of favor with the barber or his buddies, there was no telling how your haircut might turn out. I was always embarrassed after I left the barber shop. Frankly, my brothers coming out of my childhood backyard barber college had better haircuts than I received from the barbers in the seminary. Further humiliation, I was not feeling good enough, I was a poor kid. I was made to feel like a stooge, a school clown.

In the seminary, there clearly was a pecking order dictated by who was who. It was well-known who had money in their pockets, and who didn't. After all, the seminary was populated with mostly first-born kids from rich Seattleite families. News traveled fast. Were the kids flaunting their money or was I just super sensitive to the fact that I didn't have any dough? I felt uncomfortable for not being a good student and for not being first string on the ball field.

School was a lonely time. Mail call was a power play. Who received mail, who didn't, and how much mail, who received pocket money, and who would be having visitors on Sunday afternoons. If you were on the "shit list," they hid your mail. I'll never know if it happened to me. But I imagine …?

Hell, in the year I was at the seminary, my folks made one trip to Seattle to visit me. They didn't have the extra money in their budget to drive north to see me; besides, they had five other kids at home to look after three hours to the south in East Vancouver.

I was in a community "around" a couple hundred other fellow seminarians, not "with" them. I felt isolated and alone. The dining room of all places reinforced my loneliness and isolation. Since I was the only freshman student at my assigned table, I sat at the opposite end from the upperclassmen. At each meal, the food was passed from the head of the table, by the ranking student at the table. Each meal began with an upper-class seminarian giving a religious invocation from a podium elevated several feet off the floor. Wow, what power this invoked and the message it sent to those congregated in the dining room.

Once we heard the religious message to begin each meal, three times daily, another ritual followed. Every tablemate reached to the middle of their table to grab their dining napkins, each one with a napkin ring etched with their names or initials for quick identification. I didn't have a napkin ring. I learned in short order that this elite crowd had generally been born with silver spoons and silver napkin rings.

As I stretched at each meal to attempt to reach for my napkin in the center of the table, it was flung at me before I reached it. As my napkin unfurled in flight, I was embarrassed as it sailed through the air. I worked up an appetite chasing it down so that it wouldn't hit the floor, as my fellow tablemates watched and laughed at me. We're going to be priests. I thought, what is this joint?

Once we were done with the "wannabe" pope preaching from the podium and the napkin drill, it was meal time. The upperclassmen helped themselves to what they wanted to eat. By the time the serving dishes reached me, I was lucky to eat. If I had complained about those pigging out, taking more than their share, at the table in front of me or said anything derogatory, it would have meant that I would have been "starved out" for that meal, and maybe other meals to follow.

If I bellyached to a superior, I would certainly be ostracized. What did ostracism mean at St. Edward's? It meant that in the middle of the night upperclassmen would sneak into my room and haul me to the restroom and put my head in the toilet ... a flushing. If you were the victim, for the next several days you were ridiculed by all. I only made three trips in the middle of the night.

It was once again an environment where the privileged kids had privileges and the poor kids had misery. The rich kids participated and the poor kids watched. Leaving the seminary midway through the year wasn't cool. So I stuck it out.

1962–1965: High School—The Elvis Presley Years

After a year at the seminary, and a summer to think about it, I was certain that I had made the right decision. I wasn't cut out to become a priest. My goal of becoming the pope one day was a goal that I wouldn't achieve.

Now, I had to make another decision. Where would I be going to school to finish my high school education?

Even though I was no longer in the seminary, I was a still a Catholic kid. I started my sophomore year of high school at Central Catholic in Portland. My time at Central was short lived. I didn't fit in. It was clearly a fraternity for the Catholic networked families of Southeast Portland, or the better-off kids bused in from Vancouver. It felt much like the close-knit family kids who lived near Seattle but went to the seminary. I didn't have a special calling card to get me in the "in crowd"; I wasn't athletic enough or the academic sharpest knife in the drawer.

Daily, I was bused with other the kids from Vancouver attending Central. We were transported in a huge oversized-looking bus, which we dubbed the "pregnant roller skate," a bus rented from Yacolt Stage Lines. Each day, the trip to school took 30–45 minutes and what are 30-plus guys going to do on the bus when boredom sets in?

Yup, you got it. I was the target for this sport … bullying. I was vulnerable. Daily, I fought someone. My father had taught me that if you know you are going to be in a fight, to not lose, throw the first punch and make it count. One day, while riding the school bus, I was getting the best of someone by getting on top of him in the bus aisle. This person was harassing and bullying me, and I beat him up badly. As we arrived at the schoolhouse, I bolted from the bus and was greeted by the school representative, a priest who was the dean in charge of discipline. Father immediately suspended me from school for three days. I quit Central and was now on my way to Hudson's Bay High School, a public school. Yippee!

As a Catholic kid growing up, I was taught by my parents that those kids going to non-Catholic schools were destined for trouble because they were not disciplined and were too much into partying. I thought to myself, "goodie, I can hardly wait."

Trouble for me was brewing. My deportment had labeled me, maybe rightfully so, and I was now officially designated a juvenile delinquent.

After I returned to Vancouver, I returned to my newspaper selling days and made some good money.

Later, I acquired a job in a grocery store. I was no longer poor and I was truly rockin' and rollin'. I was in high school at party central with money in my pockets. Life was good.

Upon arrival at my new high school, interestingly enough my first introduction was to Mr. Earl Jackson, the Dean of Boys. He gave me the schoolhouse rules and assigned me to Mr. Len Suckling, who was to be my counselor up until my graduation in 1965. I liked this man!

My memories of that first experience in a non-Catholic school environment were the adrenaline rush—what a thrill, what a change to be in a public school. The prospects of dating, dancing, sex, boozing … partying … *à la carte* prevailed. Friday night football games were always followed by dancing and drinking at the local community center. Those of us who didn't score at the dancehall after the football games on Friday nights cruised up and down Broadway Avenue, to the dismay of the local residents and the city cops. Cruising rarely was successful unless one had some booze to offer the chicks.

My first year at Hudson Bay HS was not bad. I was academically ahead of most of my classmates because, as I had been told, Catholic kids are better educated and better students. I agree and I noticed that even though I had not been a good student by Catholic school standards, that by just being in private school I had a leg up. My year in isolation as a sophomore had some benefits; I did quite well until I found some buddies, fellow troublemakers. Once I found my "like kind buddies" the two subjects in which I was strongest started to slide. Prior to finding a girlfriend, smoking, and beer drinking, I was sharp in math and a smarty pants in Latin class.

Once I discovered the landscape and figured out the rhythm of high school, I had quite an education learning from the public school kids. The honeymoon continued as I worked my way through my sophomore year at Hudson's Bay.

As I recall my high school years, I remember mostly the events that sculpted me, not the normal focus and progression/matriculation of achieving a GPA to gain college admission, or the possibility of being a member of the honor roll society, or gaining athletic prowess as a way to obtain a scholarship. I was hustling from one job to another job, numbing out the pain of loneliness and isolation, living one difficult life drama to another.

Every night, I took home my school books, but I rarely cracked a book. On occasion, I had homework that was a must to do so that I would be able to advance to the next class level. My books looked new when I turned them back in at the end of a semester, no charge for my returned books, no dog ears.

Working at the Grocery Store

I walked in into a new grocery store that was preparing to open up down the street from our home. I went in and helped the owner set up the store by stocking the shelves. After many weeks of hustling my butt off without pay, I then received a paying job to supplement my newspaper route commissions. The owner asked me my age, I told him that I was 16 although I was only 15. Sixteen was the magical age to be on a payroll without a permit from the State of Washington. My little lie gained me employment and avoided complications.

I encouraged and allowed the guys from my high school to buy beer from me through the store's back door after dark out of sight from other than my selected beer customers. My buddies became many, but they only exploited me and in the end I paid dearly. Someone ratted on me, and the cops interviewed most of those who they knew were in the school drinking crowd. Now my grades were in the toilet, and losing my ability to buy friends through beer sales greatly increased my isolation.

So upon losing my job at the grocery store, I was a lonely guy again. The last year and a half of my high school career was riddled with ups and downs. I continued to mow lawns, deliver newspapers, paint homes, and do whatever it took to earn enough pocket money to support myself dressed in the finest of duds from The Gay Blade and Melvin's Men stores.

Since losing my job at the grocery store, I was in need of a job or two. Working at the Italian Produce markets in Southeast Portland from midnight to noon in the summers of 1964 and '65 provided me with walking-around money.

Working at the Produce Markets

At age 15, I was driving trucks for a local produce distributor at the produce markets in the same building that used to house the Lido restaurant. Each night, I would take the truck home and park it down the street next to the bus stop, where it was thought I would catch the bus to work … not far from the home with the white picket fence. I was on a path to secure my economic future through my own efforts. The legal driving age was 16 but I needed to work and Ed Link, my boss, liked my "can do" spirit. He knew that if he gave me a task it would get done lickety-split. He never asked my age so I never had to lie. To put myself at further risk it was a game going over the toll bridge connecting Washington State and Oregon State, throwing in two washers from the hardware store rather than paying the toll with two dimes. After all, twenty cents was 10% of one hour's pay at the time.

Bootstrapping was my middle name. If I wanted out of the blue collar arena and to accomplish middle class dreams, I realized I needed to pick myself up by my bootstraps and do whatever it takes to achieve success.

1964: Going to Olympia

Busted! I arrived home late one night, and my father was perched on the roof of the garage. As I pushed the window up to squeeze my way inside to my second-floor bedroom. I was told that since that I was home after midnight, only by 15 minutes, that I would need to go find a place to sleep elsewhere.

Down the street I went looking for a buddy to have some fun with. I rapped on Ron Roebeck's window, and I was told to "go away, my parents don't want me hanging out with you." But I exclaimed, I have a case of beer, you have a car, so let's go for a drive. We headed up north on the new highway, Interstate 5, drinking beer along the way. We didn't have too much to drink, just a few beers. In those days, you drank the beer and flipped the 3-cent returnable bottles along the roadway.

The escapade was going great until we decided to pull over for gas in Olympia, Washington, some 115 miles north of Vancouver. As we approached a gas station across the street from the Olympia police station, a local dishwasher, who was drunker than we were, drove through a red light on his way home from work, piling right into the front of my buddy's car. We were toast!!

The cops arrived in short order. Ron and I spent the evening in lockup, prisoners of our youthful folly. No wonder, once the police had discovered the few bottles left in our case of beer in the back seat of our car.

We were housed for the evening in the juvenile detention center. This was my first experience in the penal system, with more experiences to come. After we were shown our cells outfitted with the brightest lights I have ever seen and a ratty blanket, I had time to think. A few minutes later, I was told that my dad would arrive in the morning before noon.

I was 16, and after what I heard, I realized that I wasn't high up on my dad's priority list. The guards shared with me that when they finally reached my father at just after 2:30 in the morning he informed the police that they could throw the keys away. My father was told, you pick him up by noon, or we'll let him go free. My father and my buddy's father showed up on time at noon to escort us home.

Our fathers put a rope to the back-end of my buddy's car and the car being towed, had the banged-in front grille. It was the longest car ride of my life. My dad said not one word to me all the way home. The three-hour drive felt like a lifetime. I was wondering what would become of my future. He used the focus, to avoid talking with me, as he worked to keep the disabled car in line behind the car towing us. My father, from this memorable day forward, did not speak to me or permit me to be at the same dinner table with him for more than two years. My trip to purgatory lasted more than two years!!! I learned about conditional regard.

It didn't take a genius to figure it out. I was persona non grata at home. Frankly, life was hell. I knew that I was bad boy, but still I wanted some love. Without being loved and valued, I continued to live up to my reputation as a bad boy.

My life continued along this path of self-destruction for the next three years while I lived at home. It was just a short time later that I began driving at two in the morning when my father was working the graveyard shift. After my mother was asleep, I began to take driving lessons from my neighbor buddy, Ron. He wasn't an angel either, but he was able to get his driver's license. His parents didn't use emotional withholding to control or manipulate him. My parents did and I knew it.

With Ron as the driver, we were legal on the road but we were violating our parents' curfew and the curfew of the local authorities, not to mention the football coach's requirement that his players be off the streets by ten each school night (Ron was a football player). In the hours just after midnight, I was now comfortable teaching my buddies how to drive with me at the wheel. Frequently, when I was driving my buddies around in my mom's new, used 1959 Chevrolet Bel Air, I was so proud to show everyone my driving skills. I had many buddies who went out with me on my late night excursions (Terry's driving school). One night, I picked up Paul Stephensen a few blocks from his home, and after I felt he was ready to get behind the wheel, I pulled over and we traded seats. We left Boulder Avenue, took the first right on to Silver Star Road, and Paul took the corner a little wide and took out the first telephone pole. The car came to a complete stop. We turned off the engine and we walked home. In the morning, my mother asked me where the car was, and I told her that the car was in a wreck. I told her it wasn't my fault, that Paul was driving the car. As I left for school, the police called our home and chatted with my mom. When I arrived at the bus stop the scuttlebutt about my misfortune was already the chitter-chatter among my fellow school bus riders. The downed power line had cut off all the electricity in the neighborhood. Many people were running late this memorable day. I went to school as if nothing had ever happened. Later in the day, I was picked up at the school and taken again to the juvenile center in downtown Vancouver. This was the end of Terry's Driving School.

My teenage juvenile case was assigned to Officer Richard Karnuth. Mr. Karnuth was firm but friendly. He gave me the message. He told me, "This is your second skirmish with the law in the last two months, and if you have another one of these episodes, you will be living in the Juvenile Home along Interstate 5, in Chehalis, Washington." I was effectively put on probation. For my father, who was already not speaking to me as I had been put into the deep freeze, this all but sealed the withholding treatment and continued to feed my father hunger. I wanted so much for him to like me, to love me. I wanted his attention but he was absent and distant, and I was becoming more and more lost. My grades sank to new lows, and my deportment was in the unacceptable zone.

My 1950 Oldsmobile Coupe

My vehicle to freedom was my 1950 Oldsmobile Coupe, which I purchased from a buddy who was a fellow jailbird of mine in Olympia. This was my first car, and like everyone, I'll never forget the first car I ever purchased. This particular coupe had its back seat removed by its previous owner, turning the back seat into a bed on wheels. On many occasions, I slept there alone, and on a few lucky occasions it provided an opportunity to steam up the windows on lover's lane in the McLoughlin Heights.

Whether I was a good boy or a bad boy, I realized that I was on my own.

On occasion the Vancouver Police would show up at the wrong time, and flash their big bright flashlights right through my car's window. After the cop stared for few a minutes, he'd rap on the windows and ask us what we were up to, which signaled that it was the time for us to scoot along and carry on the party elsewhere.

1959 Austin Healy

My father enjoyed projects as part of the dream he wanted for us. He located a 1959 Austin Healy that had been in a wreck, and he was able to buy it from the local junkyard on the cheap. Between the ongoing projects and the never-ending remodeling job on our home and others, we now had another project. The car was jacked up on blocks in the front yard. This monument became the neighborhood landmark. From paycheck to paycheck we poured our money into rebuilding our newly acquired sports car to make it look like new. It was sky blue. It took us a couple of years to rebuild the car and about the time it was restored, I drove it only for a few months. After all the blood, sweat, and tears over the restoration, I went into the Army and was obliged to leave "The Blue Beauty" behind.

My Father's 19' Sabre Craft

On the other end of property at my parents' home was parked a previously owned 19' Sabre Craft boat. The boat was used for our family's annual camping and water-skiing vacations. My parents, now with six kids, vacationed every year with my mother's brother and his wife and their eight kids, my cousins. I'll never forget these trips. On my last family vacation in 1965, there were 5 adults and 14 kids, with a handful of these kids still wearing diapers. To this day when I drive by the local Oregon State Parks, I recall the time spent with my family and relatives. The boat looked well-kept, great on the outside, but on the inside the motor always needed some tinkering: a full-time vacation job for my father was to keep the motor running so we kids could go water-skiing. The harder my father worked to please everyone, the more frustrating it was for the combined camping families. These trips were so stressful, I finally used work as an excuse and never went again. To this day, I have never have had a desire to own a boat or work on a car.

High School Graduation Day

It was extremely tough stuff to see my fellow students receiving full-ride scholarships to Harvard, Yale, Stanford, and many other great schools while I was to continue to toil on the streets of Vancouver as someone not good enough to break out of the family dynamics in which I was shrouded.

My teachers had made sure that I graduated … moved along the conveyor belt to the next phase of life so as to not continue to be a troublemaker at their school. I was accepted at the local junior college, as the college was required to take all applicants from the local area.

Mr. Suckling

Mr. Suckling was a saint. Soon after he was assigned to me as my high school counselor, he became my advocate and my confessor, and he always made time for me. He expected a lot from me. I didn't measure up to the school's expectations, but he was always patient with me. He wanted me to do well in school and even though I failed my way through to graduation, Mr. Suckling was at times my only friend on the school grounds. He didn't always approve of my rock 'n' roll attitude but at any opportunity he complimented me and made me feel good. He was an "ego booster" rather than an "ego buster." We all need ego kibbles to build our ego strength.

Looking back, I wished that I had gotten to know him better. He provided for me a source of care and support. Without his efforts, I would have found my way to life at the Juvenile Home in Chehalis, Washington. He gave me hope and encouragement. Without a doubt, his ongoing weekly check-in conversations about my behavior with the authorities at the juvenile courts kept me on the straight and narrow.

November 1963

In November of 1963, we were all assembled in the school gymnasium. Mr. Paul Gutierrez, our high school principal, announced to the student body that our President Kennedy had been shot and killed. We were sent home until further notice. We learned later from watching around-the-clock television that the whole country was in shock and that America and the world would come to a complete standstill.

With the country in a funk, and no school, we high school kids had time on our hands. Everyone's parents were still working during these days of national mourning. With my girlfriend Carrol's parents at work, too, we had an opportunity to get better acquainted. Carrol and I spent the next few days at her home unsupervised. As much as I was excited to explore sex as a high school student, it didn't happen. Yes, we necked and petted, but only to a point.

Carrol and I remained a clinging couple for the next few years. In the last year before I left for the Army, our relationship became very rocky. Something was cookin' and I couldn't figure it out. Carrol was my first high school love, and I was sad to see it slip away. When I arrived in Germany, in 1967, I received a Dear John letter. Usually the girlfriend mails this letter to her military guy shipped overseas, revealing that she is now in love and having sex with his best friend, who is still living in their home town, often with, as in this case, a 4F draft status. At first, I was deeply hurt that John had stolen my sweetheart. The last I heard of John and Carrol, they have been married nearly fifty years. Happy Anniversary!

Bertram Keire

Bertram Keire is a teacher whom I'll never forget. He had clear expectations and boundaries from the get-go. On the first day of class in my senior year he set out the rules of engagement to the entire class: "These are the expectations for succeeding in this class. To graduate from school in June of 1965, you must pass this course, Contemporary World Problems." You could have heard a pin drop. Everyone in the class straightened up in their seats, no rounded shoulders, and I navigated this challenge without a hitch.

Everyone knew the rules. This very good looking teacher knew his subject matter and taught us well. He was stern as hell and serious, too. I bucked up and did the minimal amount to succeed with at least a passing grade of "C."

To create a little "high school graduation" insurance, I always offered to water and mow his yard when he was out of town. Mr. Keire was a customer on my paper route, so I knew his schedule. Whether Mr. Keire knew of my sales tactics or not, it doesn't matter, but in the end we both won. He earned my respect, he treated me well at a distance, and I received my high school diploma. His yard was always well manicured.

Graduation Celebration

My mother invited everyone she knew, her brothers and sister, their kids, my cousins, and the neighbors, too, to celebrate my graduation from high school on our newly poured concrete patio. Such a milestone accomplished, the high school graduation of a first born, was always a ready-made opportunity to weave more fabric with the relatives. Even with all the ongoing family squabbles, it was expected that at least temporarily, we would be civil and cordial during a family gathering of celebration. We were taught as children to be on our best behavior come hell or high water. This meant that we were to be seen and not heard.

With all the issues surrounding my poor grades from high school and my status as a juvenile delinquent, at last I earned my diploma. I was on my way!

I was coached that I needed to make nice at the obligatory family drill of celebration. We ate hot dogs off the barbecue, potato chips, and a yummy dessert of vanilla ice cream with chocolate sauce. As soon as I could drum up the courage, I asked to be excused and charged out that evening to connect with my girlfriend and my beer drinking buddies.

To this day, I owe several people thank-you cards for the gifts that I received. I was aware even as teenager that sending thank-you notes was the right thing to do, but the rebel in me dictated otherwise. Withholding my gratitude was not cool.

I had a diploma—not sure what it meant to me other than I would be eligible to go to Clark Junior College in downtown Vancouver, one block north of my high school.

There was a big hole; there was ritual, but no substance. I didn't hear any words of encouragement. "We love you, you will be a success"; there were never any words other than discouragement at this event or and other time. I never heard my father or my mother tell me that they loved me, or that they were proud of me.

Note from 1972

Seven years after graduation, I returned to my high school to thank Mr. Jackson and Mr. Suckling for the time they had spent with me during my high school days. Also, I wanted to apologize to them for being a bad student and a bad boy, and to let them know that I had found my way. As I entered the school house, looking for Mr. Jackson and Mr. Suckling, I passed by the many trophy cases reminding me of many missed opportunities on the athletic field. This was my first visit to the school since graduation in 1965.

Immediately, as I entered the school reception office, I was greeted and put on the witness stand by Mrs. Richardson, one of the school counselors. I remembered her from my high school days. This day led to an encounter that I'll never forget. Mrs. Richardson asked me why I was at school. Uh-oh, I thought, I'm on the witness stand. If I want a hall pass to accomplish my mission, I would need to schmooze with her. I shared with her, using a courteous tone, that I would like to visit with Mr. Jackson and Mr. Suckling. I went on to add, in my conversation with Mrs. Richardson, in my attempt at finding some warmth and a few kudos, that I had been drafted into the US Army after high school, and with the GI Bill, I had recently graduated from the University of San Francisco. She commented, with a telling tag in her voice, "Oh, you are a late bloomer." Mr. Jackson and Mr. Suckling greeted me and gave me words of encouragement. I left with positive feelings. The men were full of support, encouragement, cordial, and very friendly, and I am glad to this day that I made the effort to thank them. They are good people; we need more teachers like these two guys.

I was convinced that once I was separated from the army, I would give it my all to graduate from college.

Upon my release from the army on the GI Bill, I vowed to myself, that I would earn a college degree come hell or high water.

Civilian Life: New Horizons

Shortly after returning from my two-year military vacation in Germany, I enrolled in Portland State University. I had been drafted while living in Oregon, and at all costs I was going to avoid the dressing down that I had received from the speech professor at Clark Junior College.

As a US Army veteran I had some privileges. My scholastic standing from high school still followed me, but as a veteran, I was entitled to full admission to an Oregon State college or university. I decided to matriculate at Portland State University. Along with my admission to Portland State University, I received the benefits of the GI Bill (free medical and dental care and school expense money).

During my first six months of school, I lived with my maternal grandparents in northeast Portland. The environment was perfect. I had my own bedroom, and free board and room. Grandma did my laundry. I felt like I was living in a hotel; the service was impeccable.

Their dining room table served as my study hall desk for this now studious student. It was a good exchange; I brought some activity to their quiet home, while they spent their time watching television: Walter Cronkite, Harry Reasoner, The National Geographic documentary shows, and an occasional *Ed Sullivan Show*. Grandpa filled his days doing 5,000- to 10,000-piece jigsaw puzzles. He devoted the last 20 years of his life to putting puzzles together. I thought many times even with eyes not fully opened that he wasn't growing, expanding his world. My grandparents were stuck. I still remembered that my grandmother advised my parents not to foster any aspirations for me to become an attorney. My grandmother raised her voice to talk over Ed Sullivan on his television program, and shouted out, "Elaine, with the mouth on him, we certainly do not want Terry to become an attorney, god forbid, that we'd have to listen to him."

This time bivouacking at my grandparents was a little different too. Our cribbage playing days were over for Grandpa and me. He was now 76 years old, and had experienced a health scare. He had stopped smoking and no longer drank. No longer were there cigarettes to gamble at cribbage or swigs for me to take from a booze bottle strategically placed under every sofa cushion, or under the driver's seat in his car, and no longer was there any booze stashed in the garage.

It felt funny going to school. I was 22 years of age, an Army veteran, and a few years older than my classmates. I was a veteran at a liberal city college, where war protestors on campus took up residency. I was too embarrassed to share with anyone that I was a veteran for fear of reprisals. I quietly kept to myself. I accomplished "C" level grades and struggled through the school curriculum. I found a couple of study pals and together we plowed our way through math courses. To this day, I am grateful to Roger Yashui, a friend and fellow student at Portland State, who helped me with my studies.

While I attended school at Portland State I was able to avoid taking a speech class. However, I did run into two professors who were not kind or patient with someone wanting to make up for lost time in the scholastic department.

While I held my nose to the grindstone to do my best, both my Marketing Professor and my Finance Professor were not appreciative of my efforts. They suggested to me in different conversations that I would be better served to take back my old job at the paper mill in Wauna, Oregon. Unbidden, they told me that college was not my bag. I became further discouraged at PSU.

I recognized in the classroom that I lagged behind my school colleagues re their abilities to excel in school. However, as a vet going to school on the GI Bill, I felt that maybe since I had served my country that I would be given some encouragement by my professors to succeed in college, but to my dismay I was squelched.

Perhaps the professors were right, but the way they delivered their message and how they said it created the most disappointing days of my life. Clark College *déjà vu*. I felt that teachers and professors were a special breed, but little did I know that they too could use lessons in civility.

These guys were breathing the same high and almighty air as my neighbor Bert, who exhibited a hoity toitey attitude.

The paper mill was required by law to hold my job open for me, as a veteran, for at least a year. With this knowledge, I knew that I had a financial backup plan.

These PSU professors hurt me terribly but I continued in school this time, as I knew the next time if I were to quit school, I would be condemned to earn a living at manual labor and be paper mill bound.

The winter and spring terms at Portland State passed quickly. I was still living with my grandparents but now it was time for me to get a job after school and find a place to live on my own. I found an apartment with a classmate from my high school, Mike Wynne.

At Portland State, I continued back to school after the summer session. However, I did not sign up, for any courses to be taken from my uncivil professors.

(One civil war was quite enough, didn't need to fight another one.)

The protest riots and demonstrations continued when school continued in the fall of 1969. Even though I had my rock 'n roll attitude in check, I recognized that it was time that I find an apartment and do my own thing. As a full time student, with a job and an apartment, without grandma to do my laundry I was a busy young man. I continued to chug along through the next term at Portland State.

Connubial Bliss and Blisters

IN THE FALL OF 1969, Andi Southard and I met on a blind date. Soon after we started dating, our courtship became an interesting yo-yo. She and I were off and on about being boyfriend and girlfriend. While she led me to believe that she was interested, she was a gung ho sally, rally Delta Gamma carefree sorority gal who was in no hurry to get hogtied. She wanted to drink in all that life had to offer. Her parents supported her economically throughout her college years, and money was the least of her worries. Thank god for the invention of the VISA card, which her father paid monthly, *sans problème.*

My folks married when they were 19 and 21 years of age. I was already 23-years-old, and fully programmed to find a girlfriend, get married, and create a large clan to increase the size of the congregation of our local parish, an expectation of practicing Catholics. I'm reminded, "we are family." While I wanted the trappings of marriage and sex on autopilot, I was a poor struggling young 20-something who wanted to make his mark in the world. I was into the yin and yang of relationship territory, which I knew nothing about.

Andi and I started dating "hot and heavy." She wanted to party and dance all night and I had to draw a paycheck. While we were having a ball, I soon learned that my mill town lingo was a no go. My frequently used phrases were soon corrected. I "ain't got none," or I "had went some place," were non-starters for Andi and her friends. One day several months later, when I met her parents, I realized that my rock 'n' roll attitude, my country boy parlance, and my high school grades were on full display as they took my measure and my emotional temperature. I was not good enough for their daughter; the message was crystal clear. But who is going to tell two idealistic 20-somethings in love and sex-starved hungry tigers that they needed to cool their genes … jeans. No way.

Regardless of what anybody else thought, I represented an energetic, aspiring entrepreneur who had to work and above all else enjoyed working. Andi encouraged my aspiration to become more than a just the run-of-the-mill kid. She recognized my determination to succeed. She had her boundaries and her limits. She was patient with me, and it was her caring for me that later on would manifest her gift for me.

I knew that she offered a whole new lifestyle but I didn't realize until years later how much she risked and gave up by marrying me. I worked hard to become successful and to be influential in the community like her family but first things first, a college degree and a well-paid, launched career. I wasn't looking for an economic handout from the family but rather encouragement to go for it. Andi's parents were extremely guarded around me, it was no secret. What did I want from them? Buttoned-down Republicans from Weld County, Colorado, they were concerned that I wanted a free ride. They assumed that because I came from an impoverished background, I would be a problem and expect to be on their dole.

Andi's parents had very high hopes for their daughter to marry a blue-blood, wealthy, Ivy League-educated husband. I represented the contrast to their highest expectations. It became difficult for Andi and her parents and for me, too; I sensed *toujours* the sub-rosa undercurrent of dissatisfaction that they held towards us as a couple.

We were both young, anxious to have a mate to call our own. After we were engaged, Andi and her mother set a wedding date; December 20, 1970, in Greeley, Colorado. Now the marital logistics began. But first, I needed to find a job, I did, and to find a university or college out of Oregon to get some distance from my family. My fiancée Andi and her mother would become wedding planners. All I needed to do was to show up on the 20th of December. While the planning was in a full court press, I went to work.

Eureka, I'd found a summer job. North to Alaska, I went purse seine fishing at Excursion Inlet. I had heard that the work was tough but that the potential to make money was enormous. I soon learned after I arrived that the catch for this salmon season was bleak. I remained determined to leave Alaska with a money roll in my pocket.

After limited success at earning money seine fishing during the day, I sought out another opportunity to supplement my income. I needed to come up with another way to earn money or I would return home with empty pockets. I did piece work in the evening: an arrangement where I was paid for work completed. I nailed boxes together at the cannery and was compensated for performance, i.e., so much per completed box. I made more money nailing boxes together at the cannery, and much more than I would have made fishing, even if the season turned out to be good. Bottom line, I had money in my pockets when I returned from fishing sufficient to buy Ann's engagement ring, which she had already picked out at Greybeal's in Greeley. My gut was talking to me already. I was to go along with her good taste.

Andi was not practicing her family's Protestant faith and was a non-Catholic. Her folks insisted on a church wedding. I was a practicing Catholic when my folks were in the neighborhood or nearby. If my folks were going to be at my wedding, they decreed it had to be a Catholic ceremony. They had put their feet down on what was required for their attendance at my wedding. I got in touch with my childhood parish priest at St. Joseph's. Father Tom had been my fellow travel companion years ago to California, and he agreed to travel from Seattle to Greeley to perform the wedding. Our parents were happy; we were going to be married in a religious ceremony. On the wedding day, Ann's parents, with their huge network of family, friends, and professional associates, filled the local church. The wedding gifts of silver were piled high in my in-laws' home, it was a sight to behold. I have never seen so much silver in one place, not even in a five-star hotel.

Right after we were engaged, Andi and I chatted. We both confessed that if we were to succeed as a couple we knew that we couldn't live in Vancouver, a mill town, or in Greeley, Colorado. Her father's family was a member of a wealthy pioneer family from Greeley. My parents, as Ann discovered, were the opposite of her parents. My parents were uneducated, employed and hard workers but financially struggling, and Catholic, with many mouths at home to feed. My dad was a blue collar mill worker and my mother was a secretary. We had determined that we were to live away from my parents, with whom Andi didn't mix well, and to live at a distance from her parents as well. (Demilitarized Zone.)

Andi and her mom were always at peace with each other living in different cities. Whenever we'd visit her folks in Greeley in their home, I soon learned from my mother-in-law that after three days, guests, like fish, start to smell. She told me so. The shots at me were unrelenting. I was getting the message verbally as well as nonverbally. More squelching: now we were traveling nearly 1,000 miles to have somebody put me down, in front of my wife. Ann felt terrible but she was in a loyalty game, a no-win situation for her or for me. What is this crap, I thought. In addition to what I lacked, no college pedigree, no family "who's who" name, no career established as yet, where was all of this noise taking us? "Not good enough."

Andi's father was a Harvard-educated (Class of '41) law professor, with a successful law practice, and the owner of a huge tenant farmland enterprise around Greeley, which he inherited. Andi's mother didn't work but managed to keep herself busy with all the stuff wealthy women did in the last half of the twentieth century. My mother-in-law, who had grown up poor, was now well off. However, this did not prevent her from letting me know the road which she had traveled. She had separated herself from struggle, and she made sure that those around her knew it. I was always short on knowledge of the correct table manners, my lack of education showed, and most of all, I didn't know how to small talk. Until Ann's mother was told to knock off the scotch by her doctor, we enjoyed the same Johnny Walker Red. She did have one redeeming quality. I was always amused by looking at her smoking cigarettes with a lengthy cigarette holder. As much as she detested the politics of President Franklin Roosevelt, she mirrored him when she smoked.

Whenever I was with Andi's parents, I knew that I was out of my league. They had it all, from what I observed with an untrained eye at the time. She and her folks traveled the world. They had visited every country in the world that accepted their American passports. They both had been military officers during World War II. I never knew how much wealth they really had but one day my father-in-law exhibited a list of stocks that was long as his arm, and the list revealed all the stocks that he had purchased on the IPO opening bells on Wall Street. My in-laws were prissy-proper. My father-in-law was a nice guy, well-mannered, kind and considerate, but he never made any attempt to mentor me or to make any attempt to fill the holes in my personal fabric.

Wonderful people but clearly I was on my own to figure out my life with my wife Ann.

University of San Francisco

Looking for an opportunity to find a college where I might find a fresh start and a better acceptance by the business professors, Ann and I embarked on a mission to find another school for me to attend. When we learned that I had been accepted at the University of San Francisco, we loaded up the U-Haul, scooted down Interstate 5, and moved into a cute love nest near Market and Castro, 125 Henry Street.

The University of San Francisco accepted me as a student because I was an Army veteran and I had a sterling work record. My high school grades were nothing to write home about. However, the Admissions Officer told me that because I was a veteran, if I could get someone to write to the Admissions office about my need to work while I was a kid in high school, the school would admit me on probation. Mason Nolan, a top executive at the local newspaper company *The Vancouver Columbian*, wrote the letter that made my day, a path to graduation.

My dream of finishing college was becoming a reality. I believed that I was going to be able to wriggle my way out of the poorhouse by earning a college degree. Mr. Nolan's kind letter about my need to work and my good job performance really helped. To this day, I owe him a debt of gratitude.

Ann was well educated and she did an outstanding job of educating and encouraging me. She continued to teach and preach that my usage of double negatives in verb usage was a non-starter. She proofread my homework assignments, tutored me and encouraged me and without her help, I would not have graduated.

I graduated from college in less than three years. In addition to working odd jobs, painting homes, and working as a hotel desk clerk during the summer months and during Christmas holidays and spring breaks, I went to college full-time. I must add that as a veteran, I was able to avoid a few required freshman classes. One of them was speech, which I avoided happily.

I graduated with a 3.2 GPA with a Bachelor of Science degree in Business Administration from the University of San Francisco, in June 1972. For me this GPA was quite an accomplishment for a high school kid who was often reminded that he graduated 467 out of 505 students with a GPA of 1.67. Not a bad achievement for a kid who had been squelched with words of discouragement from previous college professors about a future in education and told to go back to the paper mill.

Ann was behind me, and her support and determination, for which I am indebted, earned my undying gratitude. Ann's words of encouragement and her academic assistance were the catalyst that contributed to my success in my quest for a college degree.

At the university, I met many students who had served in the US Army, and who had fought in combat in Viet Nam. One great guy and a good friend whom I'll never forget was Jimmy Harris. He nearly lost his life in Viet Nam. He fought against discouragement and graduated with me and our fellow veteran friends. Dave Whitfield was on active duty as a student; he was a handsome black dude, someone whom I came to know, like, and respect. Our relationship took me up market about "colorblindness," and respect for diversity, which I didn't know growing up in my hometown. Dave was discouraged too, but together we were a team. Also, I met fellow students from around the world, and hung out with these fellow travelers in academia who were from many countries: Amir from Iran, Mark from Venezuela, Francisco from the Philippines, and Francisco from Chile. The five of us were inseparable on campus. This multiplex experience was awesome at USF.

Upon my graduation from the university, Ann and I moved to Portland. Once I graduated, diploma in hand, I struggled with the question of what I would do to earn a living? My LSAT score told me that I wasn't going to be attending law school to become a lawyer. I lived up to my grandmother's wishes. "Don't let him become an attorney." Grandmother was in heaven now, so at least I wouldn't be listening to her condescending and discouraging words anymore.

Dead-End Career Move

As I was embarking on a career, I thought I would like to sell something, but what would I sell? I was reminded of my lack of a career direction when my father-in-law asked me, "What are you going to do now that you've graduated?" It was a question out of concern but already I was feeling from my in-laws that I wasn't good enough. Yes, I may have been defensive but I felt like temperature was being taken and not by the oral route. Who likes to be told through a myriad of penetrating, disguised questions that one is not well-bred and or not well-educated … not good enough? I felt sorry for myself but also for Ann, my wife. She had to endure her parents dissing me and have her parents put her up on the witness stand constantly to defend herself about my not good enough position in life. She had a father who adored her but a strong mother who was her main competitor for Bill's attention and priority.

Why not become a stockbroker? I wondered. They make lots of money advising their clients, so why not?

A few months after I graduated from college, I applied for a job as an account executive at several stock brokerage firms. Bill Roachfield, the branch manager at Dean Witter in Portland, hired me, and Ann and I immediately returned to live in San Francisco for another six months or more to study at the Dean Witter offices in the heart of the city's financial district. I passed the exam and become a registered representative … stockbroker.

Once I was out of securities school and armed with securities dealer's license I was very proud. At Dean Witter in Portland, Oregon, I worked hard cold calling people to develop a book of business. I would work evenings and weekends. I had okay success. I discovered again what I had learned at St. Joseph's Church: those who had money and were connected had a better start at building a book of business. I was learning that hard work wasn't always the answer but I had no one to mentor me.

At Dean Witter, I quickly learned that there was a class-struggle pecking order led by our branch manager. He was always asking about my birthright and socioeconomic class, while attempting to take my emotional and economic temperature. The questions seemed innocuous but were they really? Where did you grow up? Where did you graduate from? Do you know so and so? Do you ever go to Mt. Hood Meadows, Oregon, or to Sun Valley, Idaho, to ski? What kind of car do you drive? Are you a member of this club or that club? I wasn't good enough.

I have since joined the clubs they'd asked me about and have learned that what I went through was tough stuff, but I have a great basis for understanding who I am today and why.

When we returned to Portland in 1973, we set about to purchase a home. "Just looking," I said to the real estate salesman Sid Myron, but he immediately asked if we could afford $36,500. I said yes, jumping to attention; I am a veteran and have GI Bill benefits. Ann funded the down payment and we had access to a 3.79% mortgage. Mr. Myron was a very good salesman, he qualified us, and we were homeowners. It was time now to start a family. We were the youngest homeowners on Alameda Street at the time. There would be no basement to dig, no rooms to add; this home was a fully built out home in one of the nicest neighborhoods in all of Portland. I was 26 years old and on my way!

A few months after I started at Dean Witter, I cold called a client and I asked if he'd like some AA General Obligation Bonds for St. Joseph's Hospital in Bend, Oregon. He said, "Yes, I'll buy $25,000 of those bonds; our company was instrumental in building that hospital." I was proud and rushed over to tell my branch manager, and he told me that I had sold bonds to one of his clients. I said, "You haven't talked or worked with this guy in over five years."

That evening, I was so excited over my $25,000 order that I took Ann to dinner at The Ringside, only to learn from Bill Roachfield the following week that I had sold to one of his customers. He had already told me that this was the case but his reiteration of the fact was only to serve to inform me that I wouldn't be receiving the credit for the bond sale and a few bucks' commission for my efforts at giving it my all to be successful. Bill was not willing to share or to celebrate my determination to become a successful broker. Our relationship faltered rapidly. This blatant act of discouragement only furthered my resolve to become successful. He acted as if he belonged to the exclusive rich and tony crowd that was out of my reach to join. I was reminded again that I wasn't good enough.

The air went out of my balloon. I believe that Bill staged this event because he wanted me out of his office. I was going to be costing him money until I developed my own sustaining book of business. I thought he would mentor me but no, he didn't mentor anyone but his own family. He had bigshot-itis. Wishful thinking, my naiveté!

Another brokerage firm in Portland gave me a signing bonus, so I left Witter and moved across town. A few months later, I was talking to a client and the client told me that he was now doing business with Joe in my new office. I hung up the phone and I asked Joe, "What is going on?" He said, "The money is going to the same company, so what is the big deal?" I responded, "But I won't receive any credit for moving the account from Witter." I was told by Joe, that was too bad, but that he and the client go to the same Mormon Church. Another lesson learned, squelched again because I didn't have the right connections.

I should have known that the branch manager wouldn't defend me against this religious nepotism. He and Joe hung out together and were running in cahoots. And even when we went out to eat, the branch manager would order my meal without asking me for my meal preference.

As with other account executives, I was looking for the one dollar stock that would exponentially appreciate to $100 a share in a very quick time. Daily, I read all the right stuff: *Barron's, Wall Street Journal, Forbes, Fortune.* I became an expert in observing the success of other entrepreneurs, beginning with Conrad Hilton. Breaking into the brokerage business without a safety net is tough stuff.

After working for 18 months in the brokerage business, I could feel the inner pull for me to paddle my own canoe. I thought, why not go for it on my own? I'm not cut for the rules and order, and politics of big corporations, which required kissing the boss's feet even when he wasn't worthy.

The Vancouver big shots went for it, and so did Conrad Hilton; all of these guys were my entrepreneurial idols.

My brokerage client Jim Rinda had inherited a fortune from his grandfather who purchased founder stock in MGIC, an insurance company headquartered in the Midwest. Jim had a nice jump start. I liked him. He was a very nice guy who had loads of money. A call to become an entrepreneur is appealing. Becoming my own boss ... just like the big boys, became my dream.

My Business Launch Pad

THE DAY THAT I TOLD MY PARENTS that I was going to give up my new career as an account executive with the local stock brokerage, they asked me "why?" I shared my explanation of "why" since finally they had grown to accept that I was going to be a college-educated businessman who would be wearing three-piece Brooks Brothers suits, not smelly bibbed factory overalls.

I had made a significant life career change. I was now married, living in our new home, and getting ready to provide them with grandchildren, so I was okay. My mother's mother had 39 grandkids so the race was on to the Catholic Church's baptismal font.

My father had always wanted to open a business with his family name on it. I thought he would be proud of me. Beard's U-Frame. We were a build it yourself … do it yourself family. However, after sharing our business idea with my father and my mother, my father responded, "You are going to open a picture frame store, nobody buys picture frames." After more than forty years, I have never forgotten what he said. His words of discouragement struck a familiar chord with me. Once he saw that I was determined to follow my dream my father decided to help.

In 1974, at my ripe age of 26, Ann and I launched Beard's U-Frame with lots of help and advice from Ann's parents and mine. We opened our first store with $5,000 financed by the title to Ann's Porsche. My father volunteered all of his leftover time after his shift work at the mill and was always accompanied by my mother to supervise our efforts. Without my father's (and my) skill at remodeling, we would never have been able to open that first store. We worked day and night to ready the store for opening day. We were excited about the prospects of building something wonderful for the customers and for ourselves. Perhaps, we might work our way out of the poorhouse … finally!

During the next five years Beard's expansion continued. We opened ten little mom-and-pop framing stores in the Portland area.

After first opening the flagship store we did not have any customers for ten days ... things looked and felt bleak ... scary times. My wife and I were literally on our last dime, credit cards maxed-out. With a visit to the local art store we bought some paper and pens. We designed and printed 5,000 flyers, and after we closed the store each night, Ann and I, along with our beautiful German shepherd named Heidi, walked the dark streets of Northeast Portland and delivered flyers door to door into the early morning hours of the next workday. Why not, I asked, let's deliver another 5,000 flyers, and yet another 5,000 flyers ... the business took off.

Shortly after the opening of the first store, my in-laws were so curious about the business they flew in from Denver with all of their "to be framed" artwork from their ongoing worldwide travels. They used our store to do their framing. I watched as I was told by my father-in-law that he didn't need any instructions on how to use a hammer to nail his frames together. "Oh, because you are well-educated, you know my trade, too," I thought to myself. A few minutes later, I heard, "Do you have a Band-Aid?" Soon the cash register would ring. My in-laws insisted on paying full price. They knew that our success was their success. Their encouragement and support later became an opportunity that they offered to Ann and me six months after our first store opened.

My father-in-law Bill did a wonderful thing. He loaned Ann and me $15,000 plus interest on a ten-year note to open our second retail store in 1974. We paid him back in less than 12 months. That was the one and only time we did a business deal. He gave us the fishing-pole to fish with, but never gave us any fish. When I asked him to loan us some money for store number three, he said, "You're on your own." Looking back, that was a good thing.

However, my father-in-law Bill gave me some good business counseling, and I also called on my close family friend Chuck Stolz and my father. Together, we used the same business terms as when we started store number two and we launched store number three.

In the first few months of opening the first store, I was short payroll by nearly $500. I approached my father. He said that he and mother didn't have much extra money. He surprised me a few days later with the money. I told him that I would repay him in a couple of weeks. Two weeks later, I handed him back the money and he refused to take it but encouraged me to leave it in the business to make the company … a go! I thanked my father and told him along the way, in the not too distant future, I would take care of him. Our mutual understanding was all that was needed … a handshake. A couple of years later, I incorporated the business, and my father, who continued to offer me his every free moment to make the business a success, was there to build tables, fix toilets, rework the framing equipment, or improve upon the electrical; I felt that he had more than earned 10% of the company's stock.

In the midst of three store openings in 18 months, our first son Jeff was born, May 20, 1976. On the same day that Jeff was born, I met Dale Belford. Dale had an eye for and a reputation for making good business deals. He was instrumental in building out and successfully selling Farrell's Ice Cream parlors to the Marriott Hotel chain. I knew I had a winner of a company and needed some guidance. We immediately incorporated. Mr. Belford infused a tranche of dough into the business and I was now on my way. I had a real business to run, and the expectations were set high not only by me, but by Mr. Belford.

Two years later, in 1978, we were opening our ninth store; around the same time Kevin, our second son, was born and died a few weeks later of heart failure. Kevin had Down's syndrome.

During the first four years of Beards, the amount of hours that I was working each week was over the top. We had nine stores, a family, and a lot of people to lead and to manage. I had no leadership or management skills; all I knew was to keep my head down and work hard. For me everything was trial and error. The adrenaline was flowing. This created havoc for my relationship with Ann.

Looking back over the years through the rearview mirror, I realize that I was excessively focused on the business and neglectful of my marriage. I had been discouraged so much for so long, I was determined to build my business, to lift my family and me out of the poorhouse. I wanted to be somebody, a somebody I could be proud of.

During these business "start-up" times, my home life with Ann deteriorated rapidly. I was in over my head. What had worked for my parents' relationship wasn't working for me. My long work hours didn't strengthen or enhance marital bliss. With Kevin's birth, there were new daily demands placed on our relationship, and weekly counseling classes to learn how to live with and raise a Down's syndrome child. Kevin's death proved to be the last straw. Kevin's passing and my long hours at work was the catalyst for our marriage breaking up. There is always more to know behind closed doors. Ann and I remain friends to this day.

The day arrived, in March of 1981, that Ann and son Jeff drove by the Beard Frame Shops headquarters, waved good-bye, and that was it. Ten years of marriage were over. She went out of her way, as she left town with our son, to drive by my office window to honk, wave, and have me mouth a "good-bye" to Jeff. My office was where I lived; home is where I slept. Yes, she was tired of running a personal bed and breakfast with me as her only occasional client.

Ann moved to San Diego, hoping that the distance which the move created would preclude me from being in frequent contact with Jeff, and thereby out of her life, too. *Au contraire,* and much to Ann's surprise, six weeks after she moved from Portland, I began my countless trips to San Diego to see my son.

As Jeff's father, I was tenacious and persistent in my stewardship of my son. I fully accepted my responsibility as a father and over the next fourteen years I traveled an average of one to two times per month to visit Jeff in San Diego.

During this time, Jeff too, traveled nearly as frequently to Portland. I went back and forth as did Jeff regularly over weekends, and weeks at a time through his high school graduation in 1994 from La Jolla High School. The beautiful sandy beach in Del Mar, just north of San Diego, became our living room, where we spent many happy visits together.

Home alone. It was a rough and tough time rumbling around alone in our beautiful home of nearly 4,000 square feet. I worked so hard to have the trappings of success but what was success to me now? My son was no longer living with me. For Ann to have taken my son so far from me didn't seem fair. I was deeply hurt and I was again discouraged; how could someone rip my heart out? I did the best I could as a husband and a father. I worked hard to create a better life than my folks had given me. I was living the American dream, at least I thought so. Between my frequent trips to see Jeff in San Diego, and hunkering in the bunker at work, I was a lonely guy.

While it hurt to see Ann leave me and move with our son to San Diego, as the years rolled on I understood her decision to move on. I am grateful to this day for all that she gave me. She introduced me to the world of those who were educated and cultured, had class, well-travelled, and how to speak and write properly. The debt of gratitude which I owe to her will never be forgotten.

As the years rolled on, the business continued to grow. We opened several more stores, and in the spring of 1982, a fire destroyed the main offices, and the inventory at our warehouse. I was devastated. The months wore on and took a financial and emotional toll on everyone connected with the company as we worked to collect from the insurance company. I had to prove to the local authorities that I didn't set the fire, a humiliating experience. Tempers were flaring and all hell broke out.

The fire served to incite more firestorms with my family. I had been divorced only a year earlier, and I could see my life going up in flames.

A few years later, it was time again for me to stand up to speak to my colleagues at a Beard's company conference. I asked my friend Dan Skerritt to speak for me because I hadn't recovered from the less than positive evaluation of my speech at Clark junior College. Always lurking in the back of my mind were my earlier days in the second grade.

Now, the years rolling along, I was beginning to wonder how to pull my life together. I did not have the confidence to speak from the podium to my colleagues. I needed to ask someone else to do my talking. I kept asking myself what is going on. Something is not right. Once again my fears squelched me. My voice was stilled.

TheBigDay: Wedding Space

SHORTLY AFTER I CLEARED OUT MY DESK at Beard's, where I had been bivouacked for more than 25 years, following its sale to a Seattle company, I was restless for more work to do. I scoured the city of Portland to find something that would challenge me and expand my horizons. Little did I know at the time that since I sold Beard's, I had in fact said good-bye to my social net-worth … my identity in the community. Also, this heavy thought was coupled with the drive to have a sense of purpose, a *raison d'être*.

Prior to joining Rotary, my circle of friends was *très petit*. Now with the daily responsibilities of Beard's off my plate, I was free to explore and to meet more folks who were also looking to build new businesses. Start-ups! I looked at business plan after business plan. Nothing seemed to appeal to me. I was too much in a hurry to catch the internet wave.

Then one day I met Michael Cottam, who had a great idea. We carved up the equity section on the balance sheet of our new enterprise TheBigDay (a wedding-oriented internet site). We put the legal and accounting documents in place and went to work. Yes, we went right to work by rolling up our sleeves in my garage to write the code for the website, to do the admin, and all the other necessary details to set up a business.

My co-founder and I were diligently working to build our website, our new venture, with eagerness and anticipation. As members of local entrepreneur and software organizations, we were bombarded with questions from other entrepreneur "wannabees." There is no question that the excitement about our "start-up" attracted the curiosity of others. But if we would have let the questions which they asked bother us, we would have quit before we got started.

As start-up guys, we were fair game, and being naive, we were hoisted up onto the witness stand as defendants umpteen times over by curiosity seekers. The questions could best be described as disguised hostility cloaked in humor, sarcasm. To the trained ear, these barrages of cutting digs were laden with words of discouragement. Rather than helping us discover a revenue path to victory, they wolfed us with their rat-a-tat-tat drill-down unrelenting questioning. We were asked: Why are you guys doing what you're doing? Is there really a business model in what you are doing, creating and building? Again, it sounds like a great idea but how will you make money? Good content in the questions, but voices of discouragement rained in and reined in our enthusiasm.

After six months of development devoted to creating our online company, thebigday.com, the business was launched on 9/11/2001—a date, as we all know, which shall live in infamy as one of the worst days in America's history. But we were opened for business.

We struggled and we struggled with our new business model, as all Americans were doing, for months until the fog lifted on the suppressed American economy. We were wondering if we were victims of the disaster of 9/11 or perhaps we had built a company with no takers. Finally, we had a few customers trickle onto our site. We had hope.

We thought when we began building our company that we had a revenue sales model that would make every potential customer who came to our site become so filled with excitement that their socks would go up and down. Didn't happen: no surprise.

Little did some people on our team, the engineers particularly, know that when we first started the company that people don't just automatically land on our site and buy, buy, buy when the site goes live … online. They were great engineers, in a high-tech space, but a business always needs high-touch, the people. No pun intended, we were in the honeymoon space after all.

Day after day we did "what-iffing," asking ourselves will this idea or that idea generate site traffic that would lead to sales. Daily, it seemed, we conjured up a new revenue plan that caused us to flip-flop from one idea to the other. After all, I thought, we were in the honeymoon selling space with our business, and flip-flops are the things to wear on the sandy beaches. The new revenue idea became the flavor *du jour,* which gave us hope that we were on the path to victory towards revenue, which would generate positive cash flow.

There was no lack of ideas to drive top line sales from myself and others, which caused a lot of tension in the work environment. There was a huge disconnect, I knew as the experienced, seasoned, senior guy, on the team, that it takes 24/7 to produce results with a startup and that a startup is not only your work, but it is your mistress, too. We were now working to create a new company in an environment with the economy on fire; the stock market was hitting new highs, which drove our colleagues' expectations to match Wall Street paychecks. Michael and I were shooting for the moon. It was very difficult to pay movie star salaries to employees, which added to the stress levels in the company.

Finally, we hit revenue pay dirt; after nearly three and half years we found a sales stream that held promise and it did. We started off the company by selling coupons for fun "outdoor" activities for honeymooners to do on Maui, and within six months we morphed to a wedding gift registry for travel. The people who were signing up on TheBigDay registry were the same folks looking to buy honeymoon travel packages. Bingo! This discovered revenue stream generated over 70% of our top line sales and contributed 90% of our total gross profit revenue. When discouraged, keep working harder and smarter.

After another two-plus years, four years after the launching of our business, with our sales building, we were beginning to think that we might have found the secret sauce. Success!

After four years of struggling to find a revenue path, so that we could proudly hold our heads high, finally we succeeded but the tension had taken a toll on us, which made life hell. Our sagging spirits radiated throughout the community. It was no secret that we were not very happy campers in the workplace. Michael and I continued to have conversations over dinner, albeit not always an easy thing to do, but we had in common the awareness that our relationship would determine our success, which would be reflected upon our colleagues and passed on to our customers.

Our rapprochement didn't happen by accident, it was due at the time to my co-founder and me constantly taking personal inventory of ourselves, and taking an assessment of our relationship with one another. We instinctively knew that if we had a great relationship that we would benefit, and our simpatico leadership would radiate to our customers and our colleagues. We sought outside help to mediate and to ameliorate the tension between the two of us. We both shared the desire to grow ourselves, and as a result of our individual personal growth and development, individually and separately, finally after four years the company really began to take shape. The founders went to work with a real fury to engage synergistic creativity to find the business revenue streams to yield profitable results.

With honeymoon travel packages now being sold at TheBigDay and the infrastructure in place to sell travel products to honeymooners, we wanted more site traffic. We appealed to Dr. Richard and Jeff Beard, two marketing gurus, who connected with Cathy Guisewhite, creator of Cathy comics, and introduced her to the team at TheBigDay.

Dr. Richard and Jeff had read that Cathy had announced in her comic strip that she and her comic partner Irving were getting married. Yippee, Cathy signed up to use our registry services at TheBigDay. When Cathy was a guest on *The Jane Pauley Show*, she mentioned TheBigDay. She followed up after her appearance on the *Pauley Show* by inserting a mention of TheBigDay in three of her comic strips. TheBigDay's business revenue soared. Cathy raised $25,000 through her wedding registry, which was listed on TheBigDay, for her pet project, The Pet Orphanage of San Diego. The phones were ringing off the hook. A business owner's dream!

The business was now validated. However, our success attracted and bred more competition and with small margins, along with other insidious mitigating factors, the pheromones in the honeymoon online travel space raged.

What I knew from being self-employed nearly 30 years in business is that when a business starts out, most businesses go in one direction and end up going in the opposite direction before a profitable revenue, a pathway to profit, can be found and established. It takes cohesive leadership, courage, guts, tenacity, hard work, determination, devotion, dedication, conviction, and an ability to deflect discouragement … to go against the odds in the start-up world!

With the dedication of many good people who worked in the company, I am particularly grateful to my friend and fellow co-founder Michael for helping us to become a successful company. He is a top flight guy, a great software developer, and the world's best at SEO … search engine optimization. There were several people who dedicated themselves to provide the best in customer service. Thank you.

We reached nearly $10,000,000 in sales by 2006. We were eking out a tiny profit. The business was on its way to scale for us but on tiny margins, and with the entry of lots of competition, and the beginning of a deeply depressed economy, our sales slid south and rapidly.

Though living in desperate denial, I was distracted; I was in the throes of declining health. A medical event and process that we never discussed openly in the work place diverted my focus. There is *sans doute,* today, looking in the rearview mirror, that the company's leadership suffered because I was in combat one-on-one with myself.

The toll on me from what I endured in my early years, the final years at Beard's, the time that I served in bank jail, and now five years of hard-driving turmoil to create another successful business caused me to let go of the reins of TheBigDay. Knowing that I was not physically healthy, I was concerned about surviving and not about thriving.

We folded the company into another travel company near Santa Cruz, California, which felt like a good deal for all. The company to whom we sold cratered in bankruptcy April of 2009. Back to the salt mines!

Vacuum: Clean-up

AFTER A LITTLE MORE THAN 25 YEARS at Beards, I sold the company. Now that I was free from the day-to-day operations in the workplace, I took the time to reflect, to decide, what to do with my time. After grinding it out at Beards, I had a huge vacuum to fill. Working at Beards and its subsidiary companies had been for me a life of being hunkered in a bunker, since my mid-20's.

In the third quarter of life, at 52, what is it that I really want to do with my time as I looked toward the horizon. I was beginning to realize that I was only beginning to find my voice, to get up on my feet to speak with passion and confidence.

During the next several years following Beards, I would explore other business ventures, fully-engaging in a couple of companies, but my focus clearly became my mission to understand the decisions which I had made since my last "civilian" time out following my military service.

Now, I decided that I was going to live life consciously moving from discouragement to the land of encouragement and self-confidence. Yes, and to find my voice.

It took years of surfing on Dr. Richard's lazy-boy to download all the yuk that I was hanging on to. It was later that I was to learn in chatting with Dr. Richard that while moving away from Beards was challenging for me emotionally, Beards had been my life. When I sold Beards, I was selling my identity, my purpose, but I needed to move on to fill the vacuum. With what?

The next big chunk of time in my life after Beards was filled with self-evaluation, self-discovery, exploration, and adventure. Who am I, where am I, and where am I going. Not only, did I think about what I saw of my life each time I took a squint in the rearview mirror, but more importantly what was I going to do differently driving along the roads of life.

Part II

How I Found My Voice

A New Point of View

As I WAS BEGINNING TO REFLECT on my life after selling Beards, my launch pad, I started to take further inventory of myself. Moving from not good enough to I am good enough. I was an accomplished entrepreneur. I was blessed with economic success, but not feeling very good about myself or my life's direction. Frankly, I was bored and restless. I had accomplished the American Dream, I had built nearly 37-plus picture frame stores and art galleries. CASH FLOWING!!! Big Time!!!

It was time to call a professional and to seek some help. While I struggled during my first 50 years to work independently, I began to realize that I needed to work on becoming interdependent with others at work, at home, and at play.

I could feel that the drag on my spirit over the last 50 years was not normal and beginning to be harmful. I saw others having an easier time and more fun. I knew that my background had not prepared me to live a fulfilling life. I also clearly recognized that I was not the only one living in an emotional cage, but I was concerned about my particular cage.

Frequently, when I entered Dr. Richard's office, a clinical psychologist, I had many thoughts running through my head. I had a laundry list rehearsed to jam into my visits with Dr. Richard. The lists included my divorce, my difficult relationship with my parents, my business success, a new relationship that wasn't working, and what my body was telling me, plus much more. Upon meeting we immediately dove into big bucket issues which were nagging at me.

I had a college degree, had started and sold a successful business, was now divorced, living with a woman that I cared for very much, but whom I knew I could never marry. We were too different. It also seemed the more success I achieved at Beard's the larger the problems became between my parents and me. I gifted my father with 10% of the corporate stock of Beard Frame Shops without any Buy-Sell agreement. Later, I would learn that business deals not consummated in legal documentation leave one naked to the world. Generally, state laws protect minority shareholders of privately held companies. Now I understand the law, the hard way, but I was young and naïve when I gifted the stock to my father. I thought I could count on him to have my back. But he deferred to his wife, my mother. Everyone had conflicting agendas. I wanted to grow a successful company and make lots of people happy: my customers and my family. My dad wanted a chance to be recognized as more than just a mill worker condemned to the no-good pile, and my mother wanted to make all of her kids equal to each other, which would then make us a utopian family.

Bingo! I was in a cage both emotionally and financially. I knew that everything I did with the company was under their scrutiny. After all, my dad was entitled as a company stockholder. If they wanted money, they pressed me for it. They personally didn't need it, but my mother was the family Robin Hood. For her children, my siblings, she redistributed the company's wealth (and I owned 90% of the company). So, I was locked in a no-win family drama. I needed to heed the dictates of my mother in order to get along with family members who knew that I was under my mother's command. My father abdicated his decisions to my mother and reminded me that the state of Washington is a community property state. What is mine is hers and what is hers is mine.

Until both my parents passed away, I waited for some magic, but it didn't happen. I never received any encouragement, from my family or even a simple thank-you for my ongoing largesse. All I received were words of discouragement. At family holiday dinners I was lucky if anyone spoke to me. Talk about a deep freeze!! I wondered why I continually returned to be verbally abused by my family. No wonder Ann moved to San Diego. What a frickin' mess. "They write books about this stuff," I thought to myself.

My parents didn't believe in professional counseling. I was hoping that they would understand that I wanted to make amends and peace with them, that everything between us would be okay. But upon informing my parents about my seeking professional counseling, I was told that I was going over the line, they didn't believe in counselling.

Their response to my struggle for guidance was no surprise; it had been reinforced in the preceding years when my juvenile probation officer told my father that I didn't need counseling when I was in high school but that my dad did. For my father those were fighting words, and that was the last time he chatted with my probation officer.

But I needed and wanted some answers. With all the stuff that I had going on in my life, I plopped all of my rocks "on the table" at Dr. Richard's. When we met in his office, we always went right to work.

Under Dr. Richard's counseling and direction, over time I developed an internal guidance system that helped me to sort out the first 50 years of my life. Quickly I began to feel that I was getting a better understanding of who I am, and what makes me tick.

The weight of many years of unfinished business was weighing heavily on me: the lead weights were shackled to my ankles, the weights had stooped my shoulders; and the wrinkles had lined my face with excessive worry.

I was an unhappy camper and didn't even know it. Until I met Dr. Richard, and then after a few years passed, I didn't even know what it felt like to cry: my feelings had been completely numbed-out.

Later, I would learn that I was bankrupt mentally, emotionally, physically, and spiritually. Over the last few years, I had experienced divorce, the death of a son, years of loneliness and aloneness … I had nowhere to turn. I had developed the best golf swing in the world but couldn't score with it. I had made millions and lost them. My only son at the time lived in San Diego and I was commuting approximately two times per month while my business was meandering rudderless into the drink. I had girlfriends, but where was I going? I was making relationship decisions that I was ill-equipped to make … wow!

I was at a choice point. We are the product of our choices, our karma follows us. We are talking survival here folks, this was big time, and big league stuff.

Over many years, I took over 14 feet of notes that I recorded in work sessions with Dr. Richard. I went to work with Dr. Richard to shed the lead weights, and turned lead into gold.

At Dr. Richard's office, I quickly found out that I had tons of work to do, and lots of it, a lot more than I thought. So, I began to schedule a session for an hour a week, and then two hours a week, and then it became four hours per week for many years. The more I chatted with Dr. Richard, and the more books I read, the more I began to understand that I had made the right phone call. I knew that I had found the right person to help me out of a deep morass.

Now firmly committed to weekly visits with Dr. Richard, I was reading at least one book a week on psychology and biographies about famous people who have lived to make a difference in the world. Along this interesting reading trail, over a period of years, I've read several hundred books. During each session we would discuss the latest book which I had read. The book reading to supplement my therapy was a springboard to a better understanding of my issues, which I so desperately needed to sort out.

The focused and disciplined reading trail increased my vocabulary and my use of the dictionary, and it reminded me that what I was learning now at 50 years of age was a big part of what I had missed in my childhood development years. It was exciting to read, and soon a new world was opened up to me. Until I met Dr. Richard, I had been hiding in my cave at my work. He later introduced me to the opera, symphony, live theater, the blues, jazz, and other learning and cultural events.

Dr. Richard is always full of suggestions. The next move for my personal growth and development was for me to make a phone call. He knew a dance instructor whom I also had met on a cruise ship off the coast of Mexico. In 1976, Dick and Dorothy Walker were the dance instructors, and my wife Ann wanted so much for the two of us to take ballroom dance lessons but I was too bashful to take dance lessons publicly with Ann.

Why was I scared to take dance lessons? I had begun to realize that since my 6th grade teacher saw me dancing like Elvis Presley and too close to my partner, as measured with her 12-inch ruler, I had been told that I could no longer be allowed to dance at school dances. Yes, I met discouragement and again was squelched and sent off the dance floor. My lack of self-esteem contributed to my shyness and isolation.

For several months at the Walkers' home, I took private lessons from Dick and Dorothy in their basement. Dick would call the dance steps and Dorothy was my partner. I was too timid to shake my hips or to do the boogie-woogie on a public dance floor. I enjoyed spending time learning the dance moves in the privacy of their home. I rebuilt my confidence through their support and warm encouragement. After I developed confidence, I signed up for the Walkers' dance lessons that they taught to the masses. I was now dancing for the world to see. Learn to dance like nobody is watching.

Dr. Richard introduced me to community service through Rotary, which I later joined. The same year that I joined Rotary, I was encouraged to study French and then it was one new experience after another that rapidly began to expand my horizons. When he first asked me if I ever thought of learning to speak French, I was shocked, wondering why I would want to speak that language. Interestingly, in the process of learning French, my English writing and speaking skills also improved. Today, I enjoy writing, painting with words. He tricked me with his suggestion to study French. The rewards have been awesome.

I continued to seek his help as I needed coaching to become a fully built out human being. As my journey included continued visits to his office, I learned much from him: how to develop friends and relationships, the power of awareness, the value in developing a moral compass, the art of filtering those people whom we can count on for social security and those to avoid. Bottom line, he taught me how to fish, but I needed to do the fishing.

From Dr. Richard, I learned that most people would rather die than give a speech, as speech making is the #1 fear. The #2 fear is walking into a room full of strangers. The third most common fear is death. He was right on all three. I was frightened to get up and do public speaking. I was squelched in second grade and again in junior college. I needed to wriggle through the bars of my discouragement jail.

When I was 50 years of age, Dr. Richard suggested that I join Dale Carnegie Speaking Seminars and learn how to do public speaking. I thought, "I cannot believe it. How much more do I have to learn and/or re-learn?"

As I continued in my session work with the doctor, I came to realize that while my folks had no intention of harming me, their own lack of awareness doomed me to a life as a canary in an emotional cage of discouragement.

I experienced glossophobia, the fear of public speaking, so severely that I would break out in a sweat when called upon to stand up to speak. Frequently, I'd find an excuse to leave the room. I'd find excuses to hide, I asked other people to stand up and speak for me. I'd even found reasons to hide in the restrooms knowing full well that I was going to be called on to speak.

I had avoided the dance halls, too. Dancing is another form of public expression. My social anxiety limited my interaction and integration with others. Schmoozing with strangers is a form of public speaking. I avoided small talk, the traditional conversational icebreaker, which further limited my ability to connect with others.

The result: I was living a life in isolation and in loneliness.

Due to Dr. Richard's suggestion, which was a gift of helping me find my voice at Dale Carnegie Speaking Seminars and then through my active participation as a public speaker in Toastmasters, I have had an opportunity to find my flight to freedom. I have passed my public speaking enthusiasm and accomplishment on to my two sons, Jeff and MG, who now have found their voices, too.

Like many of us I was off in the business world doing my thing … too busy … for this or that … to be involved or to make a commitment. I was too busy to be a volunteer. I was too busy to make new friends and to grow. Excuses are a part of our self-imposed prison.

I attribute a great deal to Dr. Richard … a great man, a wonderful person who has guided me, and has helped me to develop my own inner guidance system.

Mom Passes: Goodbye to the General:

Family Legacy

WHEN MY MOTHER PASSED AWAY in 2003, it caused me to stop and think about our life together, what it was that we had together or didn't have together. What did I inherit from her emotionally and from my father, who passed away in 1995? What did I learn from them? What did I wish that I would have learned from them?

My parents, who have gone before me, have left their legacy and as I am writing, I'm continuing to develop and share the legacy that my sons will be inheriting. I'm living life consciously … an examined life.

What does all this mean? Why am I where I am today? Where would I like to be today and tomorrow? What will I leave behind to make a difference? Have I given my sons the tools to make their lives better?

Growing up in the '50s was much different than growing up today. In my case we grew up with phone party lines. Our first phone came with fourteen families connected to the same phone line. We had to take turns with everyone and I learned a lot from this experience about communication, and *the need to make the most of each communication opportunity.*

At my mother's celebration of life reception, I got up to share a few words of appreciation about my Mother:

I will be forever grateful to my mom and dad for giving me life … they taught me how to be self-reliant and scrappy. I had to rely on myself to build a future! My mom was duty bound in her role as a caretaker. Mom, I have fond memories of German chocolate cake, cinnamon rolls, the onion dip made with Lipton soup, and the frequent evenings at home eating popcorn. I have fond memories of Dad, too. He taught me how to make and enjoy onion sandwiches, and today I eat onion sandwiches every Sunday morning, and on special days of celebration like this one …

the celebration of your life, our life together, we start the day eating onion sandwiches.

In her sense of duty as a mom, unfortunately a rare commodity these days … she cared by care taking …

I will be forever grateful for her legacy!!!

The words that I shared at my mother's funeral reception said a lot about me and about us as a family.

My father was always working on projects to keep up the repairs and maintenance on the home … and always adding on to meet the needs of newly arrived children.

What I learned was to be self-reliant and hardworking, disciplined, focused "to get the job done, and on to the next chore." I did whatever it took because the pathway to a few minutes of freedom, indulgence, and independence was through the few dollars I would earn by collecting pop bottles left behind by the construction workers building new homes or by my delivering newspapers door to door. Not to mention I created the opportunity to buy all of my own school clothes. The neat and tidy dress served me well from the outside, but inside I was hurting and didn't know why.

Being out and about doing a variety of jobs opened the door to an awareness of what was going on in the world around me, but not with me in it, as I was always on the outside looking in as a spectator. I learned how to work but not how to be.

Curing Father Hunger

RECENTLY, WHILE CHATTING WITH MY GOOD FRIEND and counselor I was given a message that I have internalized. The message that I needed to hear was delivered softly but directly, but it has finally penetrated my mind, head, heart, and soul. It has taken me many weeks, months, and years to understand how to interpret the mail which I have received many times in the Penthouse Romper Room, where my therapy lessons took place.

Why have I lingered in this yucky chow? Because I didn't get it, I was used to eating the bad people food. Now I get it; I have spent nearly a lifetime scurrying around like a starving dog to fill a hunger pang that is a multi-generational disease handed down by my father from his father and their fathers before them. Finally, through the emotional and hurtful lesson learned that I recently received I have satisfied my "father hunger." Wow, what a relief. The fog that I have been wading through is clearing out with high winds driven with such strong force I am empowered to enjoy the clear sunny blue skies.

The lessons we learn in life are usually delivered in a painful manner and in a hurtful way unconsciously, simply due to our lack of knowledge and awareness. As Erik Erikson wrote and taught to his patients and students, when we miss a step in life, we must go back and repair the missing step in order to move to the next one.

Later we find out that we were child-like, unaware, and a bit naive to think that people were playing fair.

Looking for love and friends in all the wrong places has caused me to take unwise risks with people, which has caused me emotional stress, financial upheaval from time to time, and isolation in my thoughts and social life. But today, I am free at last, and thankful for the happiness of knowing better about whom to befriend and how to befriend and why or why not. I have learned to trust my gut.

The measure of the reward and the value of the gift of awareness is measured by the depth of our wounds. At times, we unknowingly flagellate ourselves, causing bodily harm unconsciously until we learn an all-important lesson about the step missed in our development. However, once we understand and we accept that the transgression, the trickery by others, is a valuable gift, we can consciously move on to higher ground and reap the benefits of another lesson learned. As a result, we become calmer and more powerful as we learn and grow.

As I reflect on each and every day of my life lived so far, the struggles of the past have been a gift, a bountiful harvest for me to connect the myriad of dots revealing the journey of my life, my flight to freedom. At over 60 years of age, I am now able to relive the journey which I have taken to date, and now adjust my compass with precision as to where and how I will decide where to travel, which will be more fruitful and less encumbered by the need to expect others to fill my hunger going forward. In our world of open field running, I am no longer a stray, hungry dog.

Friends are like gold, a precious few. A handful of real family, of friends to truly be "with," is sufficient to live a life well-lived, and all the other folks on the periphery are to be "around" to chat with, to share small talk and to celebrate with, but only for the occasion or the season of the gathering.

If this father hunger (and love hunger more generally) disease is not eradicated from one's being, the pain continues and it is like a cancer that breaks down the cells, the fabric of one's life, an unhealthy way to live.

Thanks, Dad, for all that you did; you did the best with what you had to work with and now it is my turn to be the alchemist. The inheritance that I received was hurtful but from my pain comes a platform of opportunity, I am grateful. No longer will others be stuffing the ballot box on my watch. In dealing with people, I trust my gut. I'm doing it "My Way!" The shackles are off and I am flying like an eagle in rarified air.

Developing Confidence is an Inside Job:

Incubating a More Positive Me

ALL THE SQUELCHING AND DISCOURAGEMENT that I experienced during my formative years left me with a legacy of a steady stream of negative self-talk. I bombarded myself with stinkin' thinking and became my own critical parent. Not Good Enough! My critical, ongoing, Not Good Enough self-talk continued to echo through my consciousness until the negative self-talk was my daily mantra, a ritual habit of sabotaging myself. I had become what I had been taught to believe that I am Not Good Enough. These negative scripts were reinforced over and over again Not Good Enough.

If I was going to stop sabotaging myself, I had to learn some new scripts, positive self-talk, an inner nurturing parent. Good Enough. Once I embraced the new script reminding me that I am Good Enough, I was launched on the inside work to regain my confidence. The more I grew my self-confidence the less I cared about what others thought of me, it was my opinion of me that counted!!!

What we think about on the inside, comes through on the outside. Once I reclaimed positive thoughts through doing away with the critical parent within me, my ability to overcome a fear of public speaking accelerated at the speed in which I believed in the new me.

Going to the podium or the lectern to give an awesome speech is more than doing deep knee-bends beforehand to loosen up, and avoiding coffee and booze, having a good night's sleep, and the practicing the speech umpteen times, before addressing the audience. The how-to books, and internet articles, on giving a great presentation have already been written, but the ability to become a great public speaker requires that we must do the work from the inside to build our confidence and self-esteem. Once we believe that we are okay than we can face the challenge of standing up and speaking out buttressed by techniques of good speech craft. The combination of a belief in ourselves and a belief in our speech material helps us to be ready to be heard, ready to face the audience and believe we are good enough!

Pascale: The French Connection

In March of 2001, Karl Koch, a friend, a fellow Rotarian, approached me as I was riding a stationary bicycle at a local athletic club. Karl asked me if I would like to meet someone. I said, "Sure! Please give me her name, phone number, and email address." I was told that it didn't work that way, and that I'd need to wait until the 21st of June, three months out. "Okay," I responded. "What is the deal?"

"You'll see."

Three months later, on the 21st of June, Karl kept his promise, and he introduced me to this very lovely and charming woman who was busy, too busy to small-talk with me, as she was serving crawfish to a hundred-plus people. I knew only three or four people at the party, while she knew everyone. I thought, how am I going to get to know this lady? She's cute and has a wonderful spirit. Her smile radiates right from her heart like I have never seen nor experienced. Wow!

Several days after we met, she was parking her car in a downtown Portland garage right next to my favorite coffee shop. I was sitting at one of the tables outside as she was making a beeline to her office. Quickly, I jumped up and introduced myself in French and asked her if she remembered me. She said, "Yes." I asked if I could call her sometime, and she said, "Yes." A few days later I called her.

We chatted on the phone as I softly started to put on the full-court press for a lunch date. I was on a mission. She responded flatly by telling me that she was too busy at work to rendez-vous over lunch. I was growing silent and thought, now what will be my next move? I thought, this cannot end in a stalemate. A few minutes later, as I was groping to prolong the conversation, she said, "I'm too busy for lunch, but we could go out for dinner sometime." The following week we went to dinner. All the books which I had read on how to date said never go out the first time on a dinner date. Already, I was breaking all the rules. I liked this gal. She did it her way.

We began to date. I was immediately taken by her *joie de vivre*. I was in awe of this gal. I was really smitten. This was the ideal lady whom I had described four years earlier to a former friend. I stuck to my guns and the universe delivered.

Several months later, in anticipation that we might live together, she put her home up for sale. This was the beginning of even more love entering my life. Pascale asked me if I would provide domicile for her little kitty named Bijou. I had never had a kitty before and I no idea what I was to do with her little kitty cat.

I quickly learned that it would be difficult to show her home to potential buyers with her little furry girl running around the house. Months later, I was to learn that if I didn't pass Bijou's sniff test, there was every possibility that Pascale and I would not have a long-term relationship.

A few days later, I had a roommate for the first time in many years. Bijou moved in and within hours she and I bonded. Bijou brought love into my home, which we enjoyed for the next 12 years until Bijou's passing. Pascale's house sold within a couple of weeks, and we were now a family of three.

Pascale and Bijou brought love into my home beyond my wildest expectations, beyond what I had ever known or experienced. Immediately, I learned from Pascale the value of unconditional love through Bijou. Their enduring relationship over the years was among the greatest gifts which I have ever received. *Bijou* is the French word for "jewelry," so appropriate.

I continue to this day to treasure the unconditional love that Pascale and Bijou brought to our home. I think of the prayer, "Lord, help me to become the person that my cat thinks I am."

Bijou passed away after 17 years. Her memory lives on in our hearts.

A few years ago, my son Jeff gifted Pascale with another kitty, a much younger kitty than Bijou; her name is Skinny. She is adorable. I am grateful to both Pascale and Bijou for having taught me that the more love I give, the more I get in return. Skinny wants to be shown affection all day long, what I do is seize the moment … *carpe diem*.

A few years later, in celebration of Valentine's Day, I'm reminded of *un billet doux* that I gave to my soon-to-be wife Pascale, nicknamed "Snuggle Muffins." Yes, the nickname is my invention.

Letter to My Wife:

Chère Pascale,

Merci beaucoup pour toutes les cadeaux magnifiques … for all the gifts that you have brought to my life … our life and continue to bring each and every day!

Each day feels like springtime, like flowers in bloom! Each and every morning, I wake up in the still of darkness snuggled up to my Snuggle Muffins, another new beginning; it quickly becomes springtime and the days are like summertime. The first hugs in the morning give me energy to begin each day anew, with renewed enthusiasm and vigor; I go after each day knowing how much you love and care for me. You send me off like a school boy feeling so proud to have somebody who really loves me.

Your compliments are like fresh bouquets each and every day. Please keep them coming! You make me feel needed, important and wanted. Up until we met, I had never experienced this feeling of true, unconditional love in my life … it is very special, *merci beaucoup*! It is the best tasting yummy people food of all that life has to offer … a pot of gold!

Snuggle Muffins, I'm looking forward to this summer to celebrating our relationship, our wedding, 23 July, at Riverwood … to share at our home which is chock-full of love, enthusiasm and a zest for life and living!

Thanks for all that you do for my two sons. They have an exceptional, an incredible role model in you … by you being you. Thanks for you being you! It is a yummy treat! *Extraordinaire*!!!

Thanks for helping me grow in a way that I would never have known without your help!

And thanks to Bijou and Skinny, too. *Bisous*! *Bises*! Kisses!

Je t'aime!

M. Très Content (M PP – Monsieur Presque Parfait)

Pascale's ongoing support of my efforts to become a better speaker ... is awesome!

She is wonderful, she coaches me in French un petit peu before I go to Toastmasters in Paris. Pascale, as a result of her efforts, and those of fellow toastmasters I am reaping the harvest of this joyride.

Why Paris: A Lust for Life:

Living My Passion

Paris started out for me as a place for a 20-something gawker to go and gape in awe at the contrast between two cities: Paris and Portland-Vancouver … the old and the new. When I was stationed in Germany in 1967, during the Viet Nam war, I felt at the time both fortunate and guilty enjoying what seemed like a government-sponsored vacation, all expenses paid including board, room, and my wardrobe.

Paris offered and continues to be a place for me to take a little break from 90-hour-plus work weeks. Paris serves as a getaway oasis and a launch pad to help me to encounter new experiences and a variety of adventures and activities, something new and totally different.

By the mid-1980s, I had already traveled several times back and forth to Paris, and then the pace picked up. I began to visit Paris twice or three times a year.

By traveling frequently to Paris, little did I consciously know that I was creating a new home and a new life and opening myself up to a world of connections many miles from Portland. In the process of repeated trips to the City of Light, Paris was becoming my second home and my country club. I soon realized that Portland is where I work and Paris is where I live and play. Now, I work and play in both cities.

I've learned that going to Paris yields a treasure trove, a wellspring of opportunity. Paris was founded about 250 B.C. Its history is old and rich; the city has many stories to tell. I enjoy digging and mining the depth of this great City. Paris is a goldmine of opportunity for those who dig a little deeper.

The Old and the New of Paris, the discoveries which I've made and continue to make, have given me the opportunity to see life in contrast from the old to the new with a history going back more than 2,000 years. This is precious perspective.

Paris is the center of the universe for many things old and new alike. The Parisian culture is unlike any other city: art, music, theatre, concerts, movies, parks, churches, historical monuments, politics, demonstrations, schools and universities, etc.

Romans founded the Parisian civilization; the City is where the greats from around the world have spent some time over many centuries and the worlds' movers and shakers continue to pour into this internationally recognized capital … *les citoyens du monde d'autour du monde.*

Monuments are many: *Arc de Triomphe, Tour Eiffel, Place de la Concorde, Place Vendôme,* etc., etc., *Notre Dame, Musée des Invalides, Le Tombeau de Napoléon, Musée Louvre, Musée d'Orsay, Avenue des Champs Elysées,* the list goes on endlessly. All these monuments and many more speak to the history and to the people and historical periods which they represent.

The Parisian style is a way of life, a lifestyle that is much different from Portland in many ways. The changes taking place currently in Portland are already baked into the Parisian socialist-capitalist society. There is an *élan* that permeates Paris like no other city, and one must go there to experience it.

Parisian personal operating styles are different from American style. The baristas at the local Starbucks in Paris do not ask ritual questions such as "How is your day going so far?" People are cordial and less intrusive in public places when it comes to queries about our personal lives.

Language: learning a new language as an adult is something which requires that we hang out in our child ego state, and exercise a sense of humor about ourselves. Through French, I've regained my childhood. I've learned from Will Rogers to laugh at myself while I'm being corrected from time to time by my dual-passported wife, Pascale, and others.

I have found that speaking another language is the greatest shopping tool in the world … a filter system second to none. FYI, the French ladies love *mon accent!* It is a handicap which I can live with … *une joie de vivre!*

There are cultural differences between the outgoing Americans and the reserved French; it is like fine wine, it takes a little time to develop close relationships with people, to delve into personal dialogs, and the treasured close friends are few.

When we take the time to learn their language and learn about their history and culture, we connect by really getting into their cultural space, and Parisians respond accordingly.

As a close friend of mine for many years, Jean Walter, a Parisian, says, "Many Americans come to Paris but few really take the time to become a Parisian." If we drink in the culture and the language, we truly experience Paris, which is reported year after year to be the most visited city in the world.

For me, Paris represents a Lust for Life … renaissance living. What does this mean for me on a deeper level? Paris continues to broaden my horizons; Paris challenges me and moves me out of my comfort zone. Making my way in a different culture and language is a confidence builder *extraordinaire.* I'm proud of the relationships which I have cultivated, and those which I am developing on a personal level. And this reaching, stretching, and growing has catapulted me into becoming more at ease in the business world.

The endeavour of studying and speaking French is beyond words and has greatly impacted me. Paris is a subject upon which I could dwell for hours. What better place might I go to *parlez en français?* After 40 years, I call Paris my other home.

Going to Toastmasters and to Rotary Club meetings serves to weave interpersonal fabric with my fellow Parisian citizens, by becoming involved in their communities.

I enjoy being a Goodwill Ambassador from the USA! I have done it so long I think the state department might want to place me on the PERS dole … Public Employees Retirement System.

Through my determination to travel back and forth to Paris to expand my world through drinking in the City, learning the language as a hobby, I have now sculpted a way of life; I have a life, a wife, a family, and a whole lot of new friends and family. *Mais oui* … and a wonderful mother-in-law, Pierrette.

Life in Paris is living a life in contrast to living in Portland, and this difference is a special opportunity.

I am able to live another life; the language and conversation give me an opportunity to plumb the depths of my soul and to take a little time to reflect … (distance gives perspective.)

Visiting battlefields in France has been a meaningful learning opportunity. More and more, I'm learning about WWI and WWII: walking in the footsteps and foxholes of our ancestors and learning about what everyone who served in battle did to fight for liberty, freedom, and the pursuit of happiness. A visit to the *Musée des Invalides* about war casualities with 60,000 objects on display will keep one off the streets for many hours.

I have been inspired by my good friend Gordon Hoffman to become more knowledgeable about the affairs of war, and how foreign wars have shaped our lives in America.

Many people flock to Paris; in fact I read a book by David McCullough, *Americans in Paris*, about Americans who flocked to Paris in the 1830s. We may have thought that everyone moved west but the *beau monde* went east across the Atlantic to Paris and London.

I have discovered that a direct report to Général Bonaparte was a guy by the name of General Bertrand. My mother-in-law's maiden name is Bertrand, and my mother's maiden name was Bertrand. I am related to the large Bertrand tribe here in Portland and in Paris.

Imagine at 46 years of age going to school in Paris with 20- and 30-somethings. I've taken French classes in Portland, in Paris, in Nice, and in Villefranche, and once in a while the classroom has been my conversation from the backseat of a New York City cab with Haitian drivers.

Over the years, I have made every intersection of French conversations an opportunity to learn more French. At the same time, I have learned what it is to be a better listener, a risk taker, a person who gets to be a kid. Whenever I speak French I am a kid.

In Paris, it is through learning French that I have found my voice. It is through the French language that I have become sensitized to the world around me to reap a bountiful harvest, to turn words of discouragement into encouragement and fly on my own wings. My world is larger and better as a result of my frequent sojourns to "La Ville Lumière."

This Too Shall Pass: A Blessed Event

MY PRIMARY CARE DOCTOR of more than 20 years was a great doctor. I always referred to him as Dr. Feelgood. When I went in for my annual exams, he would detect from time to time that my blood pressure was elevated but he thought there was no need to treat me. As I left his office each time, he patted me on the back and told me to relax a little. I always enjoyed hearing his words of encouragement. He did on a few occasions suggest that I go buy a blood pressure cuff and track my numbers. I never did. Yahoo!

Dr. Feelgood retired. Unenthusiastically, I went out on the lookout for another doctor. After all, at my age, I knew intellectually that I should be having regular physical check-ups. So, I made a visit to Dr. Routine at his office.

I was led into one of the doctor's little waiting rooms with my numbers posted on the chart. A nurse saw the BP numbers and immediately ordered a gurney thinking that I might blow up of a heart attack while visiting with the doctor. Dr. Routine was cordial, direct, friendly but firm. "You need BP meds and this test and that one, and oh yes, you need a colonoscopy, you are over fifty," he declared. The visit lasted less than 15 minutes.

I was troubled: I could feel that Dr. Routine was well-intentioned but his office staff created the worst medical environment I had ever experienced. Talk about feeling scolded, and verbally abused. I took my leave from going to any doctor's office for a few years, which nearly cost me my life.

As the time passed, I ignored little telltale signs that were showing up in my stools. Eighteen months later, I came to accept that I was living in denial and quiet desperation. I thought perhaps the red color would change and things would improve. Then one day, I received an unsolicited email from a "Dr. Smiley." I immediately dumped his unwanted email into my email trash bin. Overnight, I thought about the solicitation. I determined that this was a message from the universe, and I clearly needed to act upon it. So I called this new doctor peddling his wares, and told him that I had something going on in my body, but I would be first traveling to France and to Morocco.

As I embarked on my trip with my wife Pascale, I knew that soon after our return, I would have exams and I would know the secret that my body had been harboring. I was scared but relieved. I had been in self-imposed isolation and in mental seclusion for years with my bloody little secret, as I was to learn later.

When we returned from our trip, as promised, I went to see this smiley doctor. Yes, I would keep my appointment with him. When I arrived at his office to keep my appointment we went right to work. Small talk evolved quickly, and within minutes I shared my bloody little secret with him. He was the first person with whom I had done so. He immediately ordered up an appointment for me with a specialist at the local clinic specializing in colonoscopies, steps from the front door to the hospital. Convenient.

As I was finishing up my term as Toastmaster President, giving thanks to my Toastmaster colleagues, I was mindful that when I returned in September after our summer recess, I would be a different person.

The next day came, a Friday. I arrived at the colonoscopy factory and like everyone I was assigned to a gurney. They were backed up in a queue waiting to be wheeled along into the little room with a television monitor and a stainless steel snake-like tube ready to take a deep dive into my rear end. The procedure started, I watched the screen that was monitoring the exam, and within moments, I knew. I was given meds to help me doze off. Thirty minutes later, I was in a curtained-off room with several people waiting around my bed like I was on a death watch. As I slept the drugs wore off; I had been knocked out and now I was shocked into reality. Nobody needed to say anything. I knew. Scary.

That weekend was the longest week-ends of my life. Was I going to live, would I survive? What stage was my colon cancer? Why? How come? Why didn't I follow through and have a colonoscopy scheduled at Dr.

Routine's office a few years before? Regrets filled my mind. I was worried sick thinking that my wife Pascale might lose her husband within a year of our wedding date. These troubling thoughts, and more, raced through my mind.

What had I observed on that monitor, was it red undigested meat or the daily red wine? No, it was a report card on the stress taking a huge toll on my body by taking a big bite out of my digestive tract leading to the exit via my butt. In the next few weeks, I was to learn that I had "the poor man's disease," the result of extensive worry; my cancer was lodged and had found residency in my sigmoid colon, which is the last point of release and elimination. I was wound so tight and chock-full of toxic waste from my years of being out of sync with the universe. While living on the planet I had been holding onto voices of discouragement, which manifested itself into cancer for the uptight … no release.

Now that I had the news, surgery was my next step. I met the greatest doctor, Dr. Whiteford. His words changed the direction and course of my life. When I went to see him he was firm, friendly, easy to be with, and I left feeling encouraged that I might live. Dr. Whiteford told me to stay relaxed and if I did we could get a good result. A couple of weeks later I went in for surgery. It had been a long two weeks. Was I going to live or die? I feared for my life and most importantly I was worried about my wife Pascale and my two sons. Who would look after them once I took up eternal rest?

The day after surgery, the doctor arrived with his predictable bedside manner. He said that I was going to be okay but that he would recommend chemo for me. Damn, 3.1 stage cancer meant that the cancer had escaped outside the colon and who knows where it might spread. But I was encouraged. I was now living with regrets. I still hold the record for having been in and out of the hospital after colon repair surgery in less than 30 hours … start to finish.

Off to the chemo farm I went for the next six months. Dr. Chemo and I had another wonderful and simpatico relationship. I whizzed through chemo never missing a beat. The hours spent every other week at the farm gave me the opportunity to see how lucky I really was. Many people who were in chemotherapy around me were never going to live life past their treatment. I knew that I had a 70% chance to live at least seven years or more.

I now had a chance to change the course and direction of my destiny. I did and I did right away. I celebrated with Pascale, my two sons, and intimate friends. I contacted my personal trainer, Leno Pugh, and started lifting weights. I made a conscious decision not to discuss my cancer with anyone who was not intimately close to me. I am not into superficial love or ritual caring. I am not one to exchange small talk about my health. I shared with a handful of people my situation and I asked them to keep the little secret to themselves. All but one did. And on only two occasions have people asked me how I was doing and they did it at social events. I politely told them that I was well, and if they wanted to know more call me offline: instructing a few that they were out of bounds, and that the public arena is not the venue for taking one's emotional or physical temperature.

A year after my chemo, I started noticing neuropathy in my toes. What a funny little tingling sensation that still tingles and reminds me of my journey through cancer. Knowing what I know now I would have gone to my Chinese medicine doctor, Heiner Fruehauf, and taken his counsel and advice, to take herbs and to do acupuncture while going through the rigors of chemotherapy to alleviate the long-term effects of chemo-induced neuropathy.

While I spent time experiencing surgery, enduring toxic chemo juices, I took time to reflect and to think. I had a brush with death. But I think about Nietzsche: if it doesn't kill you it makes you stronger. Today, I am a better person for having gone through hell.

Today, when I encounter voices of discouragement I call time out. Not at this address. It has been more than eleven years since I met Dr. Whiteford. I love my red wine, a little meat on occasion, but I don't eat red beets.

Friendship Lessons

FIGHTING FOR MY LIFE AND SURVIVAL felt never-ending during 2006 and well into 2008. I was regularly spending time at the chemo farm tethered to three bags going drip, drip, drip for hours on end. One bag dangling from the medical pole tree was dubbed Fire Fox, which sounded like a program name for browser software in my laptop computer. Yes, my new buddy, dubbed Fire Fox, was going after the toxic, cancerous, unfriendly cells so as to prevent invasion of other organs in my body.

Once the regular chemo treatments were over, for the following three years I went in to see Dr. Einstein regularly at three-month and six-month intervals to check-in with him, which kept the medical event fresh in my mind. Each time I walked in for a medical checkup, I was reminded of my brush with death. Each time that I would have blood drawn, I was met at the nurses' station with a little exchange of small talk as the nursing team took my vital statistics.

This diversion from life the worst of illnesses was a gift from the universe, which gave me a prolonged period in time to really think and to process what I had been through, and why, and what I would be living with for the rest of my life. Tingling toes.

As I had much alone time in front of me, I would dwell on the past, and ponder how long I was going to live. I was all about surviving, not about thriving. During my health event, I was deep into building a company (TheBigDay) with my co-founder, who had accomplished milestone upon milestone of success. Our top line revenue was climbing rapidly, and the cash was beginning to flow.

My quiet times stimulated a myriad of thoughts about love, relationships, and a whole host of intimate thoughts. Constantly, I thought about Pascale and my two sons. I wondered how I would make my life different, healthier, so I would be able to survive and thrive to support my family. I thought about friendships, and those people who open doors for me and for others. When Pascale was on the road with her work, I was home alone, it was just Bijou, me, and CNN. I had time to think and to process things that I had done and should have done over the last 58 years, all the accomplishments and all the regrets.

After surviving the cancer bullet, I became even more direct in my communication style. My personality was exploding with glee to be free, to be alive. More and more, in an effort to develop my self-esteem and to rebuild my confidence, I entrenched myself in my Toastmaster Club. Toastmasters offered and gifted me with what I wanted and needed. Yes, the Toastmaster group provided old and new friends with a safe harbor and an environment in which to grow and develop. As a Toastmaster, I have become much more open in sharing my philosophy, my "recipe for living." I am glad that I did. I continue to do so.

With the chemotherapy treatments behind me, I realized how lucky and fortunate I am to have Pascale, my two sons, and a few close friends. However, as Sigmund Freud said, love and work are the cornerstones of our humanness. I felt good about the love department. But daily I was reminded that my work, my business, my portfolio was still going south. In the years leading up to my medical event, I had been attracting some people whom I had let in to my life knowing full well that they were not all the right people. Consciously, I realized that I needed to become the right person first, so that I had eyes to see.

With new awareness, now I needed to do some weeding of people out of my life. I had few drop-by visitors, by design, during chemotherapy. But on occasion, a friend would say I'll drop in and visit with you while you are tethered to the chemo tubes. Friends would make promises, and then some of them would not keep their promises and not show up, and not call me. Not good. Since my rebirth, those people with whom I was not simpatico have been sent to the deep freeze or took themselves out of my life.

In my thoughts, I began to plumb the depths of my soul about what friendship meant to me. The more I thought about friendship the more opportunities came to me to test me and to help me make sense out of people who are friends and who were fair-weather friends, or friends operating with expedient morality ..."self-serving."

Today, I am grateful to people who do what they say that they are going to do. People may disagree with me but I expect civility in their operating styles to hold sway, which is the pathway to mutually enhancing reciprocity. I take note of people who share their friends and their networks with me. I call these people "door openers."

Through my Toastmaster Club, I met Roger Johnson, a wonderful gentleman. At the time that I was thinking deeply about my qualifications for friendship, Roger reached out to me. What he did was a door opener of huge proportions; it sensitized and re-sensitized me to the opportunity that is extended to someone when good people share their friends, their network, and the opportunities that accompany these door openers. When a door is opened to me or to any of us, a debt of gratitude has been indelibly created.

Roger opened the door to a new opportunity, to a new world; he offered me a new network, new connections, which are one of the world's great offerings. I owe Roger a debt of gratitude for being a door opener to a treasure trove of great people.

Roger's people introductions have become the linchpin, the model, for me to take a huge inventory of the debts of gratitude that I have accumulated over the years toward many people. This opportunity for me to become more fully engaged socially is cause for me to pause and ponder how special those people are who create opportunities. The making of friendship is assisted by "door-openers."

As I was reworking my friendship garden, doing a little weeding, and sowing new seeds of friendship, I wasn't exactly done with purging friends whom I had cultivated when I was vulnerable. Over those last several months following chemo, I became an engineer: I began reverse engineering to ascertain my definition of what, for me, qualifies and defines what a friend is.

My vulnerability due to my medical event presented an opportunity for me to do some more learning. My new recognition and understanding of the value of friends, friendship, and what friends do was once again complicated by adversity. This next critical lesson learned was as tough as going through chemo treatments.

What is a friend and what is friendship? Something we Americans do not talk about, perhaps don't know how to talk about or understand its full impact. The way we interact with friends in this world is the report card that telegraphs to the world our true value system.

Friendship ranks right up at the pinnacle of the social needs list along with the significance of our spouse, partner, and/or family members. Wherever we might go in the world and connect with people, we make decisions regarding who is a friend, who will be available to develop a friendship. But yet we don't generally talk about this subject area. We discuss "who is a friend?" but do we ever define *what* a friend is so that we have clarity, a standard to take measure of a friendship? I took the time to develop my friendship filtering system.

Now I was about to learn a lesson, the hard way, with another crisis brewing in my body. Even though I had fought the good fight in the cancer prison and landed on my feet, I had another conflict waiting in the wings on the battlefield. Finally, I would learn to engage my filtering system and execute against those not playing fair ball in the friendship arena.

Shortly after I was thinking that my episode with cancer was behind me and I had faced the monster down, I was greeted with one of the worst illnesses that one may have inflicted. It is friendship betrayal. What makes betrayal hurt so much?

Several months after I had received a clean bill of health from Dr. Einstein, I received a love letter that wasn't handwritten but formal in its presentation from a friend I thought was a friend: it was a declaration of betrayal.

My gut was talking to me; I had been in denial. As it turned out, I found that this person, my friend Mr. Java, was operating by deceit cloaked in schmooze … with a silver tongue. Yes, I was inveigled with artful conversations and lured into a friendship that was grounded in falsehoods.

Now I needed to clean up the business, which was in sharp decline. Mr. Coffee, a friend of mine, had offered to help me on a volunteer basis. He knew that I had been ill, and I was under the impression that he was helping me out because he wanted to help me get back on my feet physically and financially. But he was a Rotarian, so naively I thought, I'll believe him. "Service above Self."

"Terry, I don't need a paycheck unless we hit pay dirt." "TB, I'll do anything for you, we are joined at the hips." But no, he was all about getting a paycheck, his hidden agenda. One day a few months later, he demanded a check and the love letter that I received was a lawsuit filed in court with a judgment against me for money, big bucks. I was now courting another cancer event (a social one).

This time the cancer was due to the wrong friendship. It was due to the fact that I had not defined friendship previously for myself and I was now dealing with the residue of my own unfinished business. Prior to my event, I did not have clarity about what friendship really meant, surrounded and filtered by conscious understanding of clear agendas, open and honest straight talk, coupled with integrity, honesty, loyalty, responsibilities, accountabilities, respect, clear boundaries setting, shared values, and the list goes on … expectations, obligations, etc.

When the expectations of an uplifting friendship are met we know it in our gut: our blood pressure goes down, we feel better, and we are bathed in "social security."

For friends, fidelity and mutual support provide for lasting ties and strengthening of the bond between friends. Friendship is not only a noun: it is an active verb.

Certain challenges summon friends to act in the name of friendship and require getting involved in the defense of our friend's well-being. True friendship requires an activist philosophy. If we stand on the sidelines when our friend has a need, we are not much of a friend. We need to be ready to jump into the fray, cover our friend's back, and be there to give aid and support, arm in arm.

A breach of trust, a breach of confidence, an operating style that doesn't support the expectations of a defined friendship, deceit, betrayal, silence in the face of need, idleness in the face of challenge, are among those many things which are at the root of what causes a social cancer in a friendship, what I call "gaposis."

Friendship is not taking advantage of someone who is vulnerable due to a business failure and or health issues. *Au contraire!*

There are many people who have a clear understanding of friendship and the importance it has on us in our everyday lives.

And a special thanks to that person whom I thought was a friend who has betrayed me, because in this adversity, I have something of more substance to pass on to my two sons. Their "people reads" have been catapulted up-market.

As I went through a major event a few years ago, I gained even more strength through my ordeal that now serves to empower me to restore my confidence in people as a result of having suffered so much in this terrible abyss, this pothole of deceit.

The lessons learned are enormous, and I am sharing with the world what I have learned late in life … a late bloomer in the understanding of the friendship department. I had a reason to take a pause. Yes, this preparation paperwork will go into my letters to my sons with all the details for them to see, to glean, to think about, to discuss, to process, and to learn from me these lessons about friendship.

Teachers come in many forms, shapes, and sizes. The signals are there for friendship vibes and when one is vulnerable due to a business problem or failure … if we are not careful, we'll attract to where we are and not to where we want to be and with whom we want to be. When friendship has been breached, there really is no greater hurt than when one wakes up to betrayal and deceit … at home, at work, or at play.

Rotary:

The Launch Pad for Community Service

To DR. RICHARD, I owe a debt of gratitude for introducing me to Rotary. *Voilà,* Dr. Richard found me in hiding. I was closeted at work, too busy for anything other than business. Gracefully, Dr. Richard suggested, "There is an open invitation for you to join me as a guest at Rotary." I was scared to death at the idea of going into a room full of strangers. So I manufactured reasons not to attend meetings, even though I knew that Dr. Richard would look after me. I was thinking they might call on me at the meeting as a guest, and I would have to stand up and say something. A frightening thought.

If you join Rotary, you will be asked to commit, to participate, to be involved and to be guided by the Rotary motto "Service Above Self." You will be guided and reminded of Rotary's "The Four-Way Test," and you will want to become acquainted with the ABC's of Rotary. The expectations will be high, but the rewards will be equally great. There will be wonderful opportunities to connect, to share, to associate, to affiliate, to join in fellowship with members of our club and other Rotarians *autour du monde.*

Finally, I was convinced, and I joined Rotary, to pursue goals of community service and fellowship; in the process I did discover much more than I ever hoped for. Never in my wildest dreams did I ever think that Rotary would be the opportunity to serve, to make a difference in this world, and in the process that I would be developing myself as well.

As I began my journey as a Rotarian, quickly I realized that the more I became involved through active participation in community service as a Rotary volunteer and my ongoing commitment to the goals of East Portland, Oregon, Rotary Club, the more I became connected to the service opportunity and personal benefit that is Rotary. The rewards of serving and making friends at the same time is part of the opportunity structure in Rotary. The support and encouragement of my fellow Rotarians generated the sense of excitement that motivated me to hike up my trousers and pitch in to do my share making the experience of fellowship and service a joyride … a safe harbor.

In short order, I found myself not only learning how to become a volunteer who can be counted on but enjoying the learning, doing, growing and the process of developing myself in our club. Like many of us I was off in the business world doing my thing, too busy for this or that to be involved or to make a commitment. I was rationalizing my avoidance!

Wow, I thought, what a great organization; each week these wonderful people gather around the banquet table in a spirit of fun, celebration, and service.

For many years I have been asking myself, "What can I give back to the community? Now, I ask, "Why did I wait so long?" Rotary offers the vehicle to serve others and to have a ball in the process.

The opportunity that was extended to me by my sponsor created a responsibility to be involved, to be committed, to get things done. I felt a sense of obligation and desire to make Rotary a priority. I did. I do.

As a Rotary member, I have invited scores of people to Rotary meetings who like me had been hiding in their businesses, and several of my guests got a nice whiff of Rotary and joined. Many have gone on to become leaders in the Rotary world.

Prior to joining Rotary, I knew nothing other than being alone. It was all work, and very little play, other than time with my older son when he and I commuted between San Diego and Portland. My main feelings at this time consisted of personal loneliness and a desire for connection and continued success.

Through my Rotary membership there was an ongoing bountiful harvest of opportunity to grow and connect.

During my time on the East Portland Rotary Board as a Club Member, I became more aware of the Club's fiscal responsibility to have the money in the bank before we spent it. Through the process of being a board member, I was able to clearly see the value of speaking up more and more for what is right, even when the subject on the table was not popular with fellow Rotarians.

At the Rotary International Convention in Glasgow, Scotland, in 1997, I met Jim Booth, a Rotarian, who connected me to a buyer of Beards.

Through Rotary, I was provided with an opportunity to send my older son Jeff to a Rotary leadership camp. This camping experience has had a lifelong positive impact on his development.

Each and every time a new Rotarian was inducted into Rotary, I gifted the new Rotarian with framed certificates: the "Ideals of Rotary" and the "Four-Way Test," to enhance the marketing and celebration of Rotary.

On my Rotary journey, the greatest gift of all, through fellow Rotarian Karl Koch and our mutual friend Harry Dalgaard, I met my beautiful and adorable wife, Pascale, a diamond.

As a result of my Rotarian connections, I was asked on numerous occasions to serve, and I did, on not-for-profit Boards and for-profit Boards.

I was introduced to the Arlington Club, a well-known social-business club, through two great Rotarians, Worth Caldwell and Vern Ryles.

As a Rotarian, I traveled internationally to work with people who desperately needed medical help in the outback countryside of Chile. It was on these Rotarian international missions where I met a great guy, with whom I worked in Chile, who has become a close family friend along with his wife, Ken and Christine Bloome. Friends are treasured gifts.

In 2015, shortly before Ken Bloome passed away, He asked me if I would give a eulogy at his celebration of life. I responded, "Ken, why me you know so many people."

"Terry, there will be three speakers at my service. One person will speak on my professional life, one will speak on my community service here in Santa Cruz, and I would like for you to talk about our friendship, and what friendship means to all of us."

"Ken, yes, I will, I am honored and privileged for such a high honor."

At his service. I did speak out about our friendship. I was ready. Ken had helped me to find my voice.

Voice of Discouragement: Tough Times

SHORTLY AFTER I BEGAN TO STUDY FRENCH, I was a proud *debutante* in my first year of French study, when the French professor, Sylvain, not only remarked to me in front of my classmates that I was a little off on my pronunciation but he droned on and on that I was nearly 50, and too old to really learn the French language. After having been publicly shamed, I remained in my seat and I continued to sit quietly until class was dismissed. More than ever, I was determined to learn the French language.

Again, I was squelched and discouraged by a professor. I stopped going to his class and a few weeks later, the professor phoned me and asked why I hadn't been attending to his French class.

"Professor Sylvain," I said, with a commanding voice, "I will not be returning to your class, and furthermore, I do not like being discouraged. I prefer to be encouraged when learning something new."

The conversation ended.

Shortly after this discouraging episode with my French professor, I journeyed to Paris and experienced my debut opportunity to speak in French in front of a group of people.

Finding My Voice: A Safe Harbor in Paris

As a Rotarian, a student of French, and with my schooling at Dale Carnegie I was starting to feel equipped to flex my wings. Why not, I thought, why not go as a guest Rotarian to a Rotary Club in the heart of Paris? I found an evening Rotary Club that met directly across the street from the Musée du Louvre, at the five-star Hôtel Régina.

When I signed in as a guest Rotarian at my first Paris Rotary meeting I was asked if I would introduce myself. At this Rotary meeting in this world-class hotel, I was wowed by the ambiance. As a guest, I anticipated that I would be called upon for some Rotary discussion, and I sensed with the Rotary Club officers scurrying around that their program speaker for the day was a no-show. They were a speaker short, so I knew I was going to be given the opportunity to speak. My gut was talking to me. What do I do with this once-in-a-lifetime chance? Knowing full well that I was not someone who got up to speak in public, no less in French … and if I didn't go for it, speaking in French, I would live with a huge regret. My heart, my pulse was racing.

After the club president hit the gavel to open the meeting, and completed the opening ritual, I was asked *en français* if I would like to introduce myself.

Again, what a great opportunity lofted in my direction, but what was I going to do with the public speaking chore laid out in front of me?

Thoughts were running through my head, a mile a minute. Am I good enough, will the French Rotarians understand me, will I make lots of mistakes, will they laugh at me, and will I be really good enough?

Et voilà, when asked, I gathered my strength to seize the moment and squirted up to my feet to introduce myself. I'd made my decision, which would sculpt a better life for me, and for my two sons. I had been living with quiet thoughts in my head for years, that if I didn't find my voice there was a chance my two sons wouldn't find theirs either.

One day as I looked ahead to the end of my days, I was determined that I'm not "goin' ta" wish, and regret that I woulda, coulda, shoulda develop the courage to learn how to get on my feet and deliver a speech in English … and no less in French.

The Rotary meeting hall was full of Rotarians drinking freely flowing fine wine while chatting over small talk. I was so proud to be a Rotarian to be there, all dressed up in a presidential blue suit, white shirt, cuff links, a purple tie, and spit-shined shoes, and armed with nearly two years of beginner level French.

While I was waiting to be called upon as the guest speaker, thoughts continued to pour through my head. I was aware that my French was, at best, at the advanced tourist level. There is only so much one can say to advance a conversation or a talk armed with all the tourist phrases such as "*comment allez-vous, je m'appelle Terry Beard,*" I think you get my drift, "*… je reste à d'Hôtel Duminy Vendôme*"; I was quickly running out of my French vocabulary.

Now I was being asked to stand up again to give a speech.

Finally, I had to make a decision about speaking and, if so, in English or French. French it is, I'll live with no regrets. As I spoke in French, I was sweating profusely. The perspiration was cascading off my forehead right onto my dinner plate. I spoke for nearly ten to fifteen minutes; my heart was beating like at no other time since my military days in Augsburg, Germany.

Well, I went through the speaking drill again with my limited vocabulary, "*bonsoir, je m'appelle …, j'habite à Portland, je reste à l'hotel.*" To keep me on my feet and speaking a little more, I was prompted with a question. The president of the Club asked me to explain what my Rotary Club did to make a difference in the world. I was so proud to share what our Club does in community service that the words came, to my amazement. This experience was a life-changer, a memorable and festive evening. I did it!!

As a speaker, I had been benched the last time in 1965. I had been discouraged as a student of French to give it up less than twelve months prior.

I made it through the impromptu speech *en français*, I was complimented by an 80-year-old man, who was sitting next to me, who stated that I did a very good job. Another Rotarian got up to speak, and referred to the remarks made by the visiting Rotarian. I was thinking, "this is cool."

I was further inspired by the fact that my French might not be the best tourist level French but they understood me, and being Rotarians they were gracious and patient with me. I was proud!!

Out of encouragement comes confidence and courage.

It is interesting to note, if I had spoken in English, the Rotarians would have understood me as they were all well-educated, and spoke English. Many of the Rotarians had graduated from Ivy League colleges on the American eastern seaboard.

This French Rotary moment provided me with the opportunity to do some big league life-sculpting; I went from being a shy and bashful boy, in one evening, to someone who at 50 years of age finally was able to get up in front of people to speak. All of the pent-up words of discouragement were washed from me. I had pulled up my pants and learned to take a chance to advance.

Now more than ever, I was determined, I was encouraged to continue with my studies in French. I was determined to become an accomplished English speaker and French speaker. My ex-French professor, whom I had deep-frozen, would one day know that I had quieted the demons that he created in me.

Through developing new skills like learning the French language, and in learning how to speak in public since joining Rotary, I have boosted my confidence and self-esteem.

The gifts of Rotary, public speaking, and the French language have caused me to always want to give others the opportunity to not only do community service work in Rotary but to help others to grow and develop themselves beyond where they are today by resolving their fears of public speaking, while learning another language and using Rotary as a safe harbor, a safe environment to grow and develop. The Rotary Club of Paris Alliance reached out to me and presented me with an opportunity—Frenchman Louis Pasteur said, "Chance favors the prepared mind."—this Rotary moment was a turning point in my developmental journey to move beyond discouragement to encouragement and into the land of opportunity.

It is a wonderful opportunity to overcome the fear of public speaking by becoming involved with organizations which encourage and support safe harbors.

Arlington Club Toastmasters:

The Greatest Toastmaster Club in The Universe

A few years after my French speaking debut in Paris, I was asked to join The Arlington Club, a business-social club in Portland, Oregon, in 2000.

When my friend Wake Mack spearheaded my membership into the Arlington Club, at the time, little did I know that the benefits of his strong suggestion and recommendation about me joining the Club would be such a largesse … a treasure trove. I listened to Wake, and I am eternally filled with gratitude as once I joined the club I accepted and followed his advice and became a member of the Arlington Club Toastmasters.

Toastmasters provided a safe harbor launch pad which enabled me to begin my journey to confidence and freedom from fear in connection with public speaking. I became unbound, unchained and wriggled my way out of my self-imposed cage. Getting to good enough!

Toastmasters saved and enhanced my life and became a cornucopia of opportunity in so many ways touted and described in this book. I guarantee that a group like Toastmasters can begin to free you from the chains of speech anxiety. Try it. All you have to lose are your chains of bondage. You can learn to speak up and speak out with confidence and skill!!

In the spring of 2002, I gave my first speech at Toastmasters. In Toastmasters this first speech is dubbed the "Icebreaker." This is a day which I will never forget. I was so proud to be a member of Arlington Club Toastmasters. From flunking out of junior college because the words wouldn't come, to the day when I got up to speak at the Rotary Club in Paris, I knew that I was now truly on a journey to restore my self-confidence and self-esteem with the support of my fellow Toastmasters, to become a public speaker.

On this beautiful spring day, Pascale and her mother Pierrette, who was visiting from Paris, and my son Jeff flew in from Los Angeles, and attended that early morning Toastmasters meeting. I was proud to have them with me at my first speech, my support base, but was I nervous, indeed I was. I was to give my Icebreaker. This time, the words did come, I was now baptized as a Toastmaster.

Several years later, I was asked to speak at an evening black tie event held each year by our Toastmaster Club. Immediately, I recognized Dr. Richard and Wake Mack, who were in the audience, for making this speaking opportunity possible for me.

In the speech which I gave this special evening, I shared with everyone, my lifelong companion, the fear of public speaking. I thanked everyone profusely that Toastmasters provided a safe harbor launch pad which enabled me to begin my journey to confidence and freedom from fear in connection with public speaking. I became unbound, unchained and wriggled my way out of my self-imposed cage. Toastmasters has saved and enhanced my life and became a cornucopia of opportunity in so many ways … rich and exciting.

This special evening was a moving event for me. I had prepared and given my speech without notes, telling the story of how, after many decades of hearing words of discouragement, I rose, like a phoenix, at the podium. The Toastmaster Group at Arlington Club has strengthened my positive belief in myself, validation, and today my fellow Toastmasters' patience, support, and encouragement has me believing in myself. Thank you fellow Toastmasters and guests.

This is a day which will live forever in my heart. To the amazement of most of my fellow Toastmasters, I stated that I had been on a difficult journey to find my way to the podium to speak from the heart and with openness in a way that few people live to share with such an accomplished group.

There are many take-aways for me along this Toastmaster Trail.

It takes a village to grow and develop a person. Each of us has more to learn and personal issues to resolve.

At a Thursday morning Toastmaster meeting, we heard from fellow Toastmaster Doug Houser in a speech that it took him until he was in the sixth grade to settle down and knuckle down to begin his scholarly journey.

Doug, some of us are still trying and attempting to find our footing. Doug, good for you and good for us.

While many people at our Club, "The Greatest Club in the Universe," are accomplished speakers, the mutual support and encouragement makes us all better at the podium than we ever thought that we would be and as a result better able to serve as outstanding leaders in the community.

The friendship and support that we receive from each other in Toastmasters is beyond words, it warms my heart, our hearts, and I know, we know, that we are better people for improving our public speaking skills which also enhances our confidence and self-esteem, which radiates throughout Arlington and beyond.

My gal Pascale, my best pal, frequently, I thank her for her support. As the years have flown by, I remember years ago, her words of love and encouragement before I left early in the mornings for Toastmasters is just what I needed in my early days when I was assigned to give a speech at this great club. In more recent times as my confidence has grown, her message is the same, the care is there, but now it is a little more like … get out of bed and go give them hell … tiger. As if to say, I want to sleep, so scoot. It's not the words we use but how we say them that makes a difference.

Toastmasters has helped my words to sprout wings and I thank all of my fellow toastmasters from the bottom of my heart for this uplift.

America is known to be a very competitive society and a country of rugged individualists drawing from our early days of settling the frontiers in the Wild West.

In contrast, Toastmasters is an environment, a civilization, where individuals meet collectively and thrive in harmony for the mutual benefit for the concern and welfare of one another. Playing well with others at Toastmasters is an effective pathway to become better orators.

The gift of public speaking, which Dr. Richard and Wake Mack have bestowed on me, causes me to always want to give to others. Pass it on!

Sharing Toastmasters, the rewards are awesome. There has been and continues to be a cornucopia of unbelievable returns, which yields a bountiful harvest which continues to create more defining moments … serendipitously!

I have been rewarded through my French speaking classes and Toastmasters

Experiences with the ability to speak while on my feet. Today with or without notes, because of the inspiration which I received and continue to receive in Paris and in Portland, I was and continue to be motivated and stimulated to speak more often in public.

Today it feels great to have the ability and the skills to stand before an audience and speak on matters which are important to me with passion from the heart because I have been gifted with confidence by my fellow Toastmasters. To have learned and developed a belief in myself is a huge gift of participation in Toastmasters.

Sharing this gift is one of my greatest passions … to make a difference.

Dr. Richard, Wake Mack, Paul Harris, Giselle Bawnik, The Rotary Club of Paris Alliance, The Rotary Club of East Portland, The Rotary Club of Portland, and the Arlington Club Toastmasters have reached out to me and presented me with opportunities to grow; reclaim and define myself.

Dr. Richard and Wake, I do not know if this route on my public speaking journey is what you had intended for me but this is an incredible journey. *Et voilà … nous y voilà.*

Finding my voice has helped me to assist my sons, Jeff and MG, to find theirs too. Thank you! My sons were not born with silver spoons in their mouths, but today they do have "silver tongues" in their mouths.

Today, I'm truly proud. No more glossophobia. I have found my voice and now I own it, today, tomorrow and forever.

Benefits of Public Speaking Development

The Gifts that Keep on Giving

- Overcoming the fear of public speaking.
- Confidence grows. We are rewarded with self-confidence and self-acceptance, and we gradually lose the fear of being judged.
- Become a better speaker and better writer. We become authors and story tellers.
- We become better at writing, using grammar correctly, better at vocabulary building, we learn how to say it and say it well, including; prosody, inflection, timbre, cadence, and diction.
- As an active participant in weekly meetings at Toastmasters, we not only continue to perfect our public speaking ability, speech craft, we enjoy deeper connections with fellow Toastmasters. We build a network of social connections.
- Leadership skill development—organizational training ground
- Personal insight, more self-aware.
- Sharing ourselves through personal stories – authenticity, self-revelation, transparency.
- Listen to other people speak and learn about them and their interests and get an education … personal development. "When we speak we share something we already know, when we listen we may learn something new." (Dalai Lama)
- We can learn to use humor as a social lubricant, as a way to connect with the audience.
- Social confidence. Develop the skill to "work a room" at professional and social events.

- Provides "mirroring" from an audience of supporters offering helpful feedback.
- When we write, we dialogue with ourselves, and we get to know ourselves better from the inside out.
- When we share personal stories and lessons learned through storytelling, we captivate the audience with the resulting rewards of psychic wages which restores our battered egos and feeds our self-esteem.
- The process of speech preparation sensitizes us to think about others and the impression we make when we speak. At Toastmasters, we learn to dispense with "er's, umm's, and ah's" and avoid "repeating ourselves" when we speak. When we listen to good public speakers they rarely exhibit "umm's" and "ah's" and putting sentences in reverse; backtracking; repeating ourselves is avoided.
- We nurture a community and a growing group of friends, who in turn introduce us to others. Toastmasters is an amazing networking opportunity.
- When we give a speech concerning something about which we are passionate, we become known by others as caring individuals and our messages build our inner strength which, in turn, gives us greater interpersonal power.
- We learn, through the process of speech craft, to respect other people's time by keeping our talk within the agreed upon time limit. In turn our fellow Toastmasters learn to respect our time as well. When we engage in lifelong learning and growth through Toastmasters we continue to grow and keep our youthfulness.
- Lifetime Annuity—never too early or too late to get started becoming a wonderful speaker.

Cultural Ramifications

TODAY, MORE THAN EVER, our country and the world needs a wakeup call.

Why? Most of us would rather die than be called upon to give a speech. We would rather be the person in the coffin than to be the speaker at a funeral.

The people who are frightened to stand up to speak suffer from a lack of self-confidence and a fear of being judged. Thinking "Not Good Enough." It is reputed that 80–90% of the population in the USA, suffers from glossophobia … the fear of public speaking.

In school, we are required to learn how to read, to write, to spell, and to do arithmetic, in order to earn graduation diplomas. Even at the finest colleges and universities however, students are not required to take courses in public speaking.

Many of us have engaged in sports or other competitions at one time or another. In organized competitions, we learn from our coaches to become disciplined, determined, to become organized, persistent in our quest for excellence, to excel at winning, and to become a great competitor, and go for the gold.

We learn camaraderie, we develop a sense of community, and we develop friendships which can last a lifetime. As students in grade school, high school, and in colleges and at universities, we are ensconced in a win-lose mentality on the playing field. Those of us who were not qualified to make the team became spectators, observers on the sidelines.

Professional sports are at the heart of much social chatter across the country, and television sporting events generate billions for those who are participating at one level or another. Professional sports today are a huge driver of employment, profits, and cash flow in our society.

We live in a society which is driven by capitalism which provides a culture of opportunity and as a result we have become the greatest and the most prosperous country in the world. But along the way our culture has become more of a society of exclusion than inclusion. More "me" than "we". I would like to suggest that we move to more of a "we" society. We can do this through training in public speaking-from a very early age.

Public Speaking should become one of the pillars of the academic process, transforming the 3 R's into 4 R's; **R**eading, **R**iting, **R**ithmetic, and **R**hetoric. In schools across the country, children should be required take speech classes. If we were all required to take speech classes, we would become more of a "we" society as we would be helping one another to develop self-confidence and self-esteem. We would create safe harbor environments. We would learn to talk civilly with one another. Even in debate, which is adversarial, speaking with and at one another in a civil manner should hold sway. We would all be playing at center court, on the world's stage. Peace becomes more of a possibility when people learn to talk civilly from the heart and with respect toward others.

The public speaking benefits for the individual and for society are reflected in the principles and practices of Toastmasters. When we invite young students to speak in front of their classrooms, building their strength and confidence about speaking on their feet, day after day, and week after week, we are developing our students' confidence in their thoughts and feelings and how to express what is important to them. The opportunities for teachers to compliment their students, to inspire and to motivate the students would energize the students (and the teachers!), and our society in a way that has not been felt in our country since the Greatest Generation went to center stage during World War II to save the world from tyranny and oppression.

We are the words which we speak. We must consider starting in the classrooms, at home, and at work to develop our children and ourselves and to help those around us find their voices. Parents need to converse with their children frequently, to ask their children to voice their opinions about topics being discussed and to foster a love of words; reading, writing and *rhetoric*.

We have too many Americans who are fearful of public speaking. Glossophobia is a generational legacy which is too often passed from generation to generation unchecked. Today, a privileged few, a small percentage of people, are confident in the arena of public speaking. Once we make quantum leaps with the most important currency which we exchange in our society, which is "communication," we will truly make America great. We talk about the haves and the have-nots. Do the math. Those at the top rungs of society, by a large percentage, are more comfortable with public speaking.

Unconsciously, we have become a society that puts folks on the witness stand when conversing with each other. We have moved from a society that meets and greets one another civilly to one where we are taking each other's emotional temperature and violating boundaries in the process. We as a society are engaging in conversation which borders on premature and pretend intimacy by asking personal questions before the time is right. "How's your day going so far?" Too much robotic, auto-pilot speech causes our dialogue to be stilted.

Communication is best with a little warmup of conversational foreplay. When we learn to speak with one another in a civil and respectful fashion; parent to child, teacher to student, adult to adult, we minimize soul injury and boost self-confidence. We need to incorporate the ethics of conversation in our discourse with one another.

I'm suggesting that we move toward a "we" society where we embrace civility and genuineness in communicating with one another. We must develop a consciousness-raising communication awareness modus operandi in our country. Public speaking courses for all of us will move many of us from hiding out on our porches, and up to the dais with confidence.

The art of becoming a confident public speaker needs to become a goal at home, in schools, at play, and in the workplace.

Author of "Bowling Alone," Robert Putnam, purports that we have become a society where we are "bowling" more than ever but not in leagues, we are indeed bowling alone. We are a society which has become more and more living in isolation. Communication skills give us a bridge to span the gap.

As we walk on the sidewalks, ride on the bus, taking the steps in and out of subways, or illegally texting on a smartphone while driving, we spend more time dodging one another than looking up to meet and greet those around us or with us. Our body language while we are heads down texting on the sidewalks is a form of saying, I'm taking my time in the crosswalk while showing a lack of respect and civility to the waiting traffic and a lack of availability for connection.

A focus on better communication between and among others will change our society for the better.

It is time to make these changes, and to help people stand up, step forward and speak out.

Path of Self-Discovery:

Reclaiming and Redefining

Following my first speech at Toastmasters, which is dubbed the "Icebreaker," I was on a public speaking joyride, personal journey, by conscious design to jettison the feelings of discouragement which had prevented me from getting up on my feet to speak previously. During my first speech at Arlington Club Toastmasters, I immediately recognized that I had landed in a safe harbor with friends, a coterie of like-minded people, who were giving me an opportunity that would change my life beyond my wildest imagination. Finally, I was on the path to develop myself as a confident public speaker, and with ample preparation by writing and giving speeches I would, at the same time, be reclaiming and redefining myself.

What I soon realized was that it was my fellow Toastmasters, the people, who provide the safe harbor which gave me the opportunity to work through my fears, my nervousness, and the sweat on my brow as I gave my speeches. Each and every one of my fellow Toastmasters did for me what they have done and continue to do with each other as we work as a group to become better public speakers, and for some of us to overcome glossophobia and to reap the benefits of becoming a fantastic public speaker, an accomplished storyteller.

It is always about the people. With the support and the words of encouragement to find my voice, I now own the awesome rewards which I enjoy today.

Bottom line. More than the fiats of what to do and not to do as a speaker, reclaiming and redefining oneself is greatly assisted by people who support our efforts to become better speakers. Positive self-expectations, nourished by words of encouragement, is a huge take-away from the safe harbor atmosphere of Toastmasters.

The benefits of Toastmasters are beyond belief. In the process of preparing my speeches I have been able to develop subjects and topics of interest to define what is important to me so as to live life by conscious design, I have put words to my thoughts and delivered a myriad of speeches. No longer do I hear words of discouragement from others, and through my speeches I have learned to plumb my soul to voice my values from the podium sharing about what "life" means to me. What "respecting each other's time" means to one another. The power of being actively "involved in the community" through a membership in a Rotary Club, or in another eleemosynary organization. The "words we use" and what our word choice telegraphs to others, the impact of our words is an awareness that we continue to develop. Speaking on the value of humor, the value of passing on the lessons which we have learned, and speaking on the sensitive topic such as "do people do what they say that they are going to do?" If people do not do what they say that they are going to do, there is an unacceptable gap, the distance between what they have committed to and what they have done is the gap, which we have dubbed as "gaposis". Speaking on the value of accepting and taking responsibility, the value of sharing compliments with friends and family, the value of finding a mentor, and more. These are all subjects that become part of our toolbox for communicating and making good connections. As Descartes once said, "I think therefore I am." "I speak therefore I am." Terry Beard

Reflections on Many Miles Traveled

THE ROMAN GOD, TWO-FACED JANUS, LOOKS back towards the past and forward toward the horizons of tomorrow. I can always rely on Winston Churchill to have the right thoughts and words at the ready to coach me along, urging us all to take a look in the rearview mirror if we want to see where we're going.

Today, as I look in the rearview mirror at the many miles traveled during my existence I am reminded of so much that I'm grateful for: at home, at work, at play, and out in the community.

While traveling to Paris, I discovered and dove into a book entitled *The Secret*. The book got me thinking about life and I was reminded that life is not a dress rehearsal and that what one pours oneself into usually happens, becomes manifest.

During my many years on this planet, I've had to learn tough lessons, and at times I've developed a little scar tissue in the process. I am motivated to leave a legacy behind and leave this world a little better than I found it.

Today, I look back, and see that I've created my launch pad to opportunity. I endeavor to truly live a conscious life worth living and to avoid at all cost living a life driven by my subconscious … on autopilot.

Living a conscious life is living life, a life crafted, drafted, and executed from my own design, my life blueprint.

For me on a deep and powerful reflective level, it is evident that I have had my share of struggles as well as many, many gifts and good times. As I enter my dotage I have realized that life may pass by quickly like a thief in the night, which has generated a sense of urgency in me. I truly recognize that our existence on this planet is fleeting and I must be all that I can be and become—and NOW.

Even with all the squelching that I have experienced, I get up each morning with a feeling of gratitude which determines my altitude so I can fly high in this world and soar ever closer to my lofty goals.

What I find precious is that I continue to work to evolve to become a better person, a better friend, a better husband, a better parent, and a better ambassador to the citizens of the world.

Living life consciously continues to give me opportunities to take risks to develop, to learn to reach out so as to stretch and grow. I am grateful for the support, for the fellowship and community of our universe, which is life's school house.

For me, I'm going to continue to make every meal a feast, as I have my own private French chef at home, make every day a holiday, every night a party, every yesterday a precious memory and every tomorrow an exciting adventure on the horizon. I invite you to join me in this questing. *Carpe Diem!!*

Part III

Speeches

A Sampling of Speeches Delivered at a Variety of Venues

Wet 'n Wild

As a volunteer at a local prison facility, I am frequently reminded of the value of humor and its importance in holding the attention of a captive audience. This morning, I am going to share with you the observation that guys who are locked up and dressed in prison denim and even those of us who are not housed behind bars or doing hard time can have a very good time with humor and levity. When we share self-deprecating humor it warms up the atmosphere and creates an environment which brings down the walls of physical and emotional imprisonment.

In January of last year, my friend and fellow Toastmaster, Paul Laskonis, asked me if I would assist him a couple of times a month with a community service project. I said ... "Sure, what do you have in mind?" Paul responded. There is a Toastmaster Club in NE Portland sandwiched between Columbia Edgewater and Riverside Country Clubs. The Rose City (RC) TM Club is an inmate TM Club at the Columbia River Correctional Institution (CRCI) which meets each Wednesday afternoon, from 2:15 to 3:45P, and the TM Club is looking for a couple of volunteers. I agreed to give it a shot. I liked what I was hearing and decided to take the risk. Why not, it had been 50 years since I had been behind bars in Olympia, WA.

Since Paul and I began working at CRCI RC TM, the number of TM inmate members has grown from a handful to a packed house. Currently, there are 20-25 inmates in attendance each week plus two or three volunteers at each meeting including the Head Prison Honcho Miss Popov and CRCI's Program Director, Fabian Dorgan.

I could go on all day long about what the experience is like for Paul and for me as TM volunteers at CRCI. However, today, I am going to share what we have all learned from Will Rogers ... the value of self-deprecating humor.

A few weeks ago, at a TM meeting at CRCI we were one speaker short. Miss Fabian Dorgan, the Program Director, raised her hand and volunteered to give a speech, her first one to the TM inmates. What I am going to share with you was a life sculpting moment for me and everyone else in the room who listened with rapt attention to Miss Dorgan as she gave her speech. We hung on to every word.

Now that we have a speaker, we need an evaluator. The TM inmates were reluctant, I surmised, to raise a hand for fear that they might lose accumulated time off for their good behavior due to a less than positive evaluation. I thought, I'll do the evaluation, I have nothing to lose. She can't bust me.

As the TM program wore on, I was looking forward with eagerness to hear Miss Dorgan's first TM speech. My fellow TMs were thinking the same thoughts, I'm sure. Anticipation was in the air and one could feel that everyone was wondering what is this gal going to say to this captive audience … me included. Frankly, I didn't know what to expect of Miss Dorgan. Up until this moment, she had only spoken a few words at Toastmasters.

Our third speaker was finally introduced by Toastmaster Paul Laskonis. Paul exclaimed. And today, our third speaker is Miss Dorgan, she is going to speak for 5-7 minutes and the title of her speech is Wet 'n Wild. Folks, let me tell you, the crowd went wild. Is this lady going over the top or what?

The inmates looked at one another and at me, we all locked eyes and laughed our fannies off. All of us were riveted to our seats and we hung on to every word this lady spoke. Miss Dorgan spoke for nearly eight minutes and her speech was flawless. She spoke up, used gestures, used her voice to draw us in. We laughed and rolled in the aisles for the full duration of her speech. Go girl go! We all had forgotten that we were in residence at the local big house. The inmates and staff walking by outside the meeting room were peeking in the windows wondering what is this lady doing in there with the Prison Director Miss Popov and 20 plus jailbirds. We were oblivious to what was going on around us or that we were all behind bars and bullet proof glass. There might be 580 other male inmates down the hall in various housing units but right now we are glued to Miss Dorgan's riveting speech. I haven't seen so many people laughing this hard in years.

You see … Miss Dorgan is a queen size lady. Her speech is a personal story which is a page out her family scrapbook. The speech is about an experience 20 years ago when she took her 11-year-old daughter to Las Vegas to escape the summer rains of Portland.

As planned by Miss Dorgan's daughter, mother and daughter each packed their swimming suits. Miss Dorgan confided that she hoped to avoid wearing her suit. Shortly after arriving at their hotel in LV and upon looking outside from the hotel room balcony her daughter spotted a huge sign which read "Wet 'n Wild (a water park)." The outside temperature is 115 degrees. There was no way that she could tell her daughter "no."

Miss Dorgan hoped after they arrived at the hotel, that she would be able to put on her suit cover up with a towel and quickly jump in to the hotels pool. But no, it wasn't going to happen. They were off to Wet 'n Wild, the local swim park with wading pools, swimming pools outfitted with open slides and see through tube slides filled with water.

After paying for an all-day pass for two, immediately mother and daughter headed over to climb the 15-foot ladder to slide down inside the "see through tube."

This captive audience was already roaring with laughter at the imagery which Miss Dorgan had given us but the best was yet to come. As she spoke, we all exchanged laughs and chuckles with each other.

Miss Dorgan steps to the side of the podium points to her hips and says we are now climbing the 15-foot ladder, with my daughter in front of me, and all I can do is imagine what the other swimmers behind me must be thinking as they are looking up at my butt which is as large as the state of New York. With that scene firmly fixed in our minds, all of us in the big house cracked up. There wasn't a dry eye in the room.

The story goes on. Finally, her daughter slides quickly through the tube to a large wading pool at the bottom. Now Miss Dorgan takes her turn and frees herself from the ladder's handrail as her daughter cries out, "come on mom, it's your turn." Within seconds upon letting go of the handrail she finds herself hopelessly stuck in the water tube.

OMG!!! The play park employees and everyone in the park found their way to this ride at Wet 'n Wild. Miss Dorgan was the star attraction as she was stuck in the tube. The fire department and the police sirens were drawing unwanted attention to the lady stuck in the tube. Just exactly what Miss Dorgan was hoping to avoid, all the attention that she was receiving by wearing a swimming suit, and being stuck in the tube. This story goes on and on, we are laughing like we've never laughed before. Miss Dorgan's story and her way of sharing her worst fears had us all hanging on to her every word. After nearly 30 minutes she was washed free with thousands of additional gallons of water being forced down the tube to free this by now frantic wet and wild lady. Her daughter continues screaming, "Mommy, hurry come on down the water is really warm." "Mommy, you can do it!"

As Miss Dorgan finally oozes out the tube into the freeing waters she discovers that she has lost her suit during her transit through the tube to freedom. Miss Dorgan gives us the details again, that her butt is bigger than the state of NY, and we roar some more. She grabs a towel and hugs her daughter! And she says, OMG!

My turn comes to give my evaluation of Miss Dorgan's speech.

"Miss Dorgan, you hit the ball out of the park with the bases loaded. That speech was incredible. Once again, the captive audience roars with laughter. I went on with my evaluation which really served no purpose; she truly scored and connected with everyone in the room.

So I switched gears, I picked up on the vibes in the room. I experienced how humor helps us to forget our problems and where we are relishing the moment even while serving time in the big house.

Miss Dorgan's speech provided an atmosphere in a joint where everyone melded and bonded together like I never thought that I would experience particularly behind bars. Miss Dorgan is a kind and gentle lady but she deals with and works in a tough crowd. Her well told Wet 'n Wild speech had given her credibility as a great speaker and as a human being. The captive audience had come to appreciate her talent in sharing her sense of humor. She earned more respect from my TM inmate colleagues. She and the inmates in the room had shared a moment which will have them all connected in a special way for however long they have to serve time in the joint.

A sense of community, connectedness, and levity as a result of this speech by Miss Dorgan served to show the value of humor and the value of being a great Toastmaster.

This speech has inspired and motivated me to share it for many reasons. It urges us all to become consumers and vendors of humor in the service of having a humorous outlook on life even when times are tough … serving hard time.

These guys in lock up are doing time for their misdeeds in society but they too are human and deserve and are entitled to experience levity while doing hard time. They are in jail to serve time. They are physically and emotionally in jail, and when humor is injected it lowers the anxiety levels which these guys sorely need and helps them feel more connected with prison buddies with whom they share laughter. It reduces the stress on the prison staff and makes life better for all of us.

Miss Dorgan has spent over 25 years in the prison system and recently left the Big House in Salem to work at CRCI. The time which she spent in Salem was with the prisoners on death row.

After Miss Dorgan's speech, she is now taller than the state of New York. The Toastmaster inmates love her. They are connected through the prison system in way which they never expected. With the evaluation which I gave her she and I are now connected. Imagine this, every time I go to CRCI, I now receive more than the perfunctory handshake from a prison official but I get a huge hug and a big kiss. Imagine what my fellow TM inmates think when they witness that intimacy which I now share with Miss Dorgan.

Thank you Will Rogers and Miss Dorgan.

Attitude of Gratitude

ON THANKSGIVING DAY EACH YEAR, we are reminded of an "attitude of gratitude" and the practice of saying "thank you" more often to those towards whom we feel some gratitude. Too often we take each other for granted and fail to say what we feel. Sharing "thank yous" with people who have made a difference in our lives is like giving a verbal bouquet. A gift that benefits both donor and recipient warms the heart of those who receive and elevates those who give. Thank yous are inexpensive, always in stock and easy to offer once we develop the habit. Operating with an attitude of gratitude creates a rising tide of good will which lifts all ships. It sets a good example for all who observe and interface our behavior and inspires others to follow our example when we lead with gratitude. Let's make Thanksgiving Day last all year long and often. Only once a year makes us a turkey, let's make every day Thanksgiving and let's make every day a tribute to the value of living with an "attitude of gratitude".

As we all think about our legacies, in the attitude of gratitude department, the question arises about how we want to be remembered. As a parent, I'm constantly reflecting on what I will leave behind for my two sons; Jeff and MG. They are young men and nearly every day I receive a thank you in verbal form expressing their gratitude. These *billet doux* arrive frequently in the form of a thank you note. In fact, when I receive a wave of snail mail notes, and emails of thanks, and text messages, which all represent flower bouquets, they warm my heart and make me happy and very proud to be their father.

Whether I'm at a coffee shop, a grocery store, an airline ticket counter, and at many other places of business, or at an event as a member of a forum or organization, I'm shocked by what I witness and experience. An attitude of gratitude seems to be on the decline. The days of people greeting people with a friendly welcome, "Thanks for coming today, how may I help you." Or simply, "Nice to see you." Those days are long gone from the history book of service styles involving expressions of gratitude.

Frequently, I am asked by family and friends the cliché question, "How is your day going so far?" and other such ritualized questions. When my mom was in critical care two years ago bleeding out from an ulcer. I took a break and chased down a cup of coffee, and as I walked into the coffee shop, I was greeted by, the ritualized greeting, "How is your day going so far today?" To many of us this is a charming greeting, but quickly I felt as well-meaning as this person from behind the counter may have intended to be the choice of words left me feeling a little violated, someone was taking my emotional temperature, and attempting premature intimacy at a sensitive time.

The words we choose have impact. We need to be responsible for the consequences of the words that we speak. We all need to raise our awareness level about the impact of what we say and how we say it and be able to benchmark our utterances and feel proud of our chosen speech craft. Hopefully, we all operate with some level of "Social Interest," that is caring and concern for our fellow man. Words can hurt or words can uplift, words can inspire, words can deflate. The speaker needs to choose the loving message, care about consequences of impact via word choices and practice intentional communication that is like offering a beautiful bouquet.

Let's craft our messages so as to avoid mindless speech and help our country move towards more thoughtful and genuine dialogue. We want to express gratitude in the expression of thank yous, don't delay it, say it. As we become more mindful of our attitude of gratitude in our appreciation of one another and work to enhance uplifting communication we'll be rewarded, as our attitude of gratitude will determine our altitude.

Pull up your Pants, Take a Chance to Advance, Go to France and do the Dance

In the process of continuing to improve my French, I have had some of the most memorable times of my life. This stitch in time may never repeat itself quite the same, *bien sûr*, for sure.

After several years of studying French in Portland and in Paris, I was feeling ready to spread my wings. After surveying the terrain I spotted an opportunity to fly, to soar to higher heights. I speak French beyond tourist level and have given speeches in French in Paris at Rotary Clubs and at Toastmaster Clubs. However, I knew that I wanted to advance my French speaking skills, so I took a chance. I attempted during a four year stretch to gain enrollment to *à L'Institut de Français, à Villefranche, France,* on the Cote d'Azur between Nice and Monaco.

The school is situated high up on the hill on the *moyenne corniche,* next village over is Cap Ferrat, which is the nicest and most picturesque and expensive real estate in all of France.

Each and every time I attempted to gain admission into L'Institut de Français, I was turned down. I learned that the school is filled up … booked up way in advance. Later, I learned that the repeating students, recurring revenue, is more than 25% of each enrollment period. Nice report card. So I was told. "Monsieur Beard, we'll put you on a waiting list." I've been there before, done that one. "Hurry up and wait"

Last March, the Executive Director of Alliance Française, Portland Chapter, Linda Witt wrote an article about her experience attending school at L'Institut de Français for the Portland Alliance Française monthly bulletin. Wow, I thought, okay, good for her. Immediately, I sent Linda a celebration card and told her that one day I'd like to go to that same school. Before signing hugs and kisses to the congrats card, I asked if she might know anyone who might be a "door opener" for me to gain admittance to the school. Two days later I received a call from Linda. If you are ready to go, you are in. "I just spoke with the Director of the School Frédéric Latty." Would you like to go in September or October? I said let me check with Pascale, my wife. My wife serves on the Board of the Alliance Française, Portland Chapter, with Linda Witt.

Pascale said, "goodie," you and I have been wanting for you to go to this school for a good long time. Can you be gone that long from work? I said, yes, *et tout de suite j'ai dit* … right away, I said, September works better for me. Quietly, I thought, the weather is perfect for jet skiing on the Mediterranean.

I plopped down the deposit for school. I was committed. I was willing to take a chance to advance.

A few days later, I was having breakfast with Linda's husband Hans Witt. He congratulated me on my enrollment in the L'Institut à Villefranche. He gave me an email address with which to contact Susan Bromwich, the real estate "go to" person in Villefranche. Right away, I contacted Susan and another deposit later, I had reserved an apartment beautifully appointed, a 500 sq. ft. apartment with a 200 sq. ft. balcony overlooking the Mediterranean for the entire month of September. Thank you, Hans! Friends help each other to gain the keys to the kingdom. Freedom and opportunity!

The days, the weeks and the months passed. I was eagerly anticipating my departure for six weeks in France. But as the time approached, I began to question myself. Can I really be gone this long to study French? What are the real benefits? *Je me demande … pourquoi?*

Finally, I rationalized that going to school for a full month would never occur at the optimum time. But I must go. With support from my wife Pascale and from my colleagues at work. I was free to go and embrace an opportunity which I created and was able to execute because I had support. Everyone was championing and supporting the risk, the chance which I was taking … to advance *mon français.*

With school starting in a few days, it was time to catch an EasyJet flight from Paris to Villefranche and go to school. I arrived at the Nice airport, taxied over to my home for the next month and had the week-end solo to think about the decision which I had made to go to school. I realized that

I was doing a good thing, I was not going to be living in a rut, and I had been following my gut to follow through on taking a chance to pull up my pants to advance in France.

I was excited and eager to see how my first day of school was going to go. I knew that I would be in for a battery of testing, written and oral by native tongue speaking French professors. At my age, I was thinking who needs this stuff. Evaluation, placement, correction on proper grammar usage, *bien sûr* from time to time instructive advice how to better pronounce some words, but I sucked it up, pulled up my pants and engaged my child ego state. My laughter was the talk of the L'Institut, everyone commented that they loved my laugh. Teachers who were still in class rather than telling me to keep my laughter down closed their classroom windows to the chuckles among my colleagues and me. (Laughter gives birth to smiles, first in French and then in English.)

I knew by attending school in Villefranche that I was in for the ride of my life. Indeed, I knew that by taking a risk I was going to be writing another great chapter in my life. I did. Thank you school chums!

The first day of school. We spent all morning being thoroughly tested, and I was placed in a group with others at my level. No surprise!

In the afternoon of the first day, it was all about what to expect as a student at the L'Institut along with the do's and don'ts at the school house. Rule #1. After the first day, English was not allowed at any time. We spoke French from 8-5 p.m.. Total immersion.

Once school got underway I felt like I was in high school, everyone was meeting one another and arranging meetups … dinner dates. The red wine flowed nightly. Believe me folks, I thought that I knew networking and how to do it. This was networking at its highest level. Rolodex diplomacy.

Going to school, classroom work, general assemblies, dining at breakfast and at lunches together, forming dinner groups, pétanque parties, movie going parties, and individual students hosting receptions in their apartments. I hosted too. It was fulltime rock 'n roll.

The School cooked-up many opportunities for all of us to connect, to bond and to make the most of our school days and evenings, too.

Friday night of our first week of classes, the cafeteria was closed at 5P and we were all invited to return to a school dance from 7-10 p.m.. Our cafeteria was now the dance hall. The caviar, the grub, the champagne and the wine flowed. *Imaginez!*

I had ants in my pants so I asked Katy to dance, she is 25 and lives in Washington DC and then I found myself dancing with many other gals from 25 to 85. I found a dance with Sarah, 85 years old, from New Zealand, an accomplished watercolor artist. She was a level one debutante. She too took a chance to advance, and took a dance with me. *Imaginez!*

I decided many years ago to get off the sidelines and on to the dance floor of life.

Thank my lucky stars that years ago I took a chance to advance. At the school in Villefranche, I did indeed get a chance to dance, with ants in my pants, with my fellow classmates with those in their early twenties, to those in their mid-eighties. Thank you Linda Witt! "Chance favors the prepared mind!" exclaimed mon ami Louis Pasteur.

Often times after school we'd run into fellow school chums in the village along the promenade on the seashore at bars and restaurants. Everyone was alive and on fire … with life and learning. We were at adult camp.

80 students were enrolled. 25% of the enrollment at the school was folks over 55 years of age. There were 17 countries represented in the schoolhouse student body. My daily classroom colleagues included; an Australian, a Dutchman, a Russian gal, a Canadian, and three Americans.

Of the many folks in the school I got to know a number of them. Barry Aling from London is an entrepreneur who lives between London and St. Maxime-St. Tropez. Pascal Ris is a bartender who works between Amsterdam and Antibes. Perry Gotsis is a doctor who lives between Naples, Florida and New York City; Ann Fishman lives in New York City, a marketing guru; Con Way Ling sold his last business ten years ago and currently, he is working on his next gig; Paulette Bourgeois lives in Toronto and to date has sold, over 65 million children's books; Edward is a big time writer from Atlanta, Matthew is a graduate student from Toronto. The list goes on. Mark from Australia lives and works for the United Nations in Geneva. But what was important, was not just their successes and accomplishments which we learned about each other for four weeks during and after school.

It was a bountiful harvest, a feast of people of all ages coming together to take a chance to advance. It is interesting to note that 65% of the student body was female. Who needs eHarmony?

Each of us was required to give at least one speech in French. I was ready, did one and did another even though I wasn't asked to do an encore. A fellow classmate heard my speech on entrepreneurialism and afterwards asked me to chat about Attensa, an online research solution company. He made an investment in Attensa. Thank you Con Way!

As it turns out, Linda, my sponsor to the L'Institut, and her husband Hans Witt were vacationing in Villefranche, so my buddy Con Way was introduced to Hans the COO of Attensa. I didn't go to Villefranche to raise investment money. But when Con Way approached me I pulled up my pants, and said, "Why not, here is another chance to advance." Multi-tasking. Thank you, Con Way!

It was great fun to have Hans Witt in the neighborhood in Villefranche, vacationing. Pascale and Hans' wife Linda entertained each other while Hans and I talked shop. We did lots of dinners together and often times with my school chums. Pascal, Barry, Perry, Con Way, Valerie, Jeff, Paulette, Elena, Thomas, Scott, Ann, Kim, Katy, Sarah, and I drank up most of the good red wine. Villefranche is Party Central. Hans and I are saving some of the red wine for next time when we return to Villefranche, Chez Betty, and for me and some others back to the schoolhouse.

At the end of September, my wife Pascale joined me in Villefranche. I had seen her last in Portland in late August. It was great to see her and to share with her my new life…as a schoolboy. She is great! She liked my deep tan and my new reading glasses from St. Tropez … Club 55.

I took a chance to advance in France.

I went to Villefranche to enhance *mon français* and in the process I learned more about myself.

I spiked my French skills, my public speaking skills, met new and interesting people from … *autour du monde*. Made some new school chums. I've connected with a several new friends. Linda, my sponsor, and my wife Pascale witnessed me in the school house having a ball schmoozing *en français.* I've contributed by inspiring Linda's husband Hans to learn a little French. *Pourquoi pas?*

The last day of school. Two p.m. sharp. It was my turn to have a private session with my professor Evelyne to review my progress for the month. Who went with me? My wife Pascale. She and I sat in little student chairs across from the professor at her desk and she gave a complete run down on my progress while in school to my wife. OMG, thank god I understand French. I truly felt like I was in high school sitting next to my mommy. I was truly in my child ego state … loving every minute of it. The love and the caring! It was all about me. Pascale came away knowing full well that I was a good student, committed, determined, focused, and was welcomed as a returning student next April. I was indeed a good schoolboy.

More than ever I am convinced that it is always good policy to take a chance to advance. Life is not a dress rehearsal. Laugh out loud, who cares, don't be afraid to make mistakes speaking a foreign language and to have people giggle at themselves. Be open to others and new experiences, and people of all ages will flock to your door, here in the USA or in France…*ou autour du monde. Court newness. If we always do the same old thing, the same old way, we won't grow and we will begin to wither away.*

When it was Toastmaster time at the L'Institut, as required by all students, I was ready, not scared, because my fellow Toastmasters in Portland have given me the chance to advance by speaking in a safe harbor. I was prepared. No notes, I spoke from the heart *en français. Merci mille fois!*

Whenever you have a chance to do something new and different as the late Paul McMahon, a member of Arlington Club Toastmasters, always said, take that chance. When you do new and different things it creates and expands a life. It might be our last chance to dance.

Dr. Richard, you suggested 15 years ago that I study French. You believed in me. You took a chance that I would advance and now I'm off to the next dance.

In Villefranche, it felt like floating in heaven, I never heard anything uttered other than words of encouragement and I went to France to take a chance and now I can feel the difference it makes to advance.

It's Never Too Late!

50th Reunion Invited Speech

To BORROW A PAGE from Lou Gehrig's book ... I am the luckiest person alive.

It is an honor for me to be asked by our High School Reunion Committee to speak to you for a few minutes this evening.

We have all been on a journey, we found the sidewalks, the school buses, the carpools to high school, and 50 years later we are looking back on our individual and sometimes very different journeys which we have all traveled to bring us to this moment.

Over the last year, I have attended many of our class' reunion committee meetings. However, there was one meeting I missed and when I attended the next meeting, I was told that I had been selected to be the keynote speaker this evening. A lesson about the importance of being a regular attender.

Thank you!!

During the last several years, I have been taking pen to paper and have written a manuscript. Writing the manuscript was and continues to be a wonderful exercise in looking in the rearview mirror at the choices which I have made. Sans doute, all of us have been reflecting as we celebrate here this evening.

For me the high school experience was memorable. Many times, like many of you, I didn't feel good enough. I knew that I was quick, a good newspaper boy rain or shine, not studious, didn't study, couldn't dance, couldn't get up on my feet to speak, and I had a rock 'n roll attitude which didn't comport with expectations of our high school teachers and my fellow classmates, in class or in the school yard. So as the grades came in they didn't bode well for me, or for my future. Tough stuff being a juvenile delinquent.

Thank you, Gary Huss, you took the risk with Mr Allinger with your classy operating style which kept me in school on the conveyor belt to graduation. I am forever grateful to you. You assured Mr. Allinger that if he, Mr Allinger, would permit me to be in his senior class "Home Room" with you that you would make it your personal responsibility to take me under your wing as your younger brother. Gary, you provided me with an opportunity, and I didn't disappoint you nor me.

Judy Jendry, thank you, we continue our friendship to this day by touching base frequently over the phone or via email. You were among my best ever study hall buddies. We use to yak a lot and we still do.

Diane Kessler … study hall

Michelle Halsworth … math class.

To all of you, like all of you, we have many memories to share with one another Which have shaped our lives so far.

What is the greatest, the biggest lesson which I have learned since 1965? "It is never too late."

The grades which I received at Hudson's Bay were reflected in my senior class standing. I graduated 467/505 with a GPA 1.67. Until recently, never did I think that I would be so bold as to showcase my accomplishment.

It is never too late.

When we graduated in 1965, we were all at a major choice point.

Do we go to work, go to college, use the scholarship package, get married, have a family … etc.

As we look back at our high school graduation, 50 years ago, … it was a time for a new beginning for all of us.

With my class standing, #467, I clearly knew that I only had one academic option available to me, Clark Junior College.

Our local junior college was obligated to accept me as an incoming freshman in the fall of 1965, regardless of grades, because I was a citizen of Vancouver, Washington. Besides, I already had a social security card issued years ago with my name on it, a tax payer, and Washington State Driver's License. On June 30th, my 18th birthday, I registered for the US Draft.

In the fall of 1965, like all of you who attended Clark College, I was required to take a speech class. When my turn came to give a speech, I stood up on the dais to present my first speech since second grade. (In the second grade, I had been benched.) I knew this day was do or die for me. I prepared my speech about my newspaper-sponsored trip to Mexico City, and what the trip meant to me as a young lad growing up poor in Vancouver.

As I stood up to give my speech; I shook like I had never shaken before. I quaked in my boots. If I didn't pass muster at the podium I was surely going to soon be wearing combat boots, courtesy of being drafted into the US Army.

At the podium, I was totally embarrassed and humiliated in front of everyone, the words just wouldn't come, and I was petrified. The final blow came when the speech teacher said in front of the class, that in all of his years of teaching, I had given the worst speech he had ever heard in one of his classes. I realized that maybe he was right, my speech was not very good, but why should I be so beaten up in front of people?

Devastated, immediately after being berated in front of everyone, I quietly left for the college bursar's office to withdraw from school. I had flunked out of junior college. I asked for the refund percentage of tuition to which I believed I was entitled, but to no avail. I missed the deadline to receive a refund on my tuition by one day. I was in and out of college in less than four weeks, perhaps a world record.

I was frightened, I was scared, and I had no one to chat with, no one to console me, to guide me, to help me sort out my feelings, my life. I was alone. I had a terrible relationship with my parents; they had no time for me. My parents didn't know what to do with me or how to help me with my growing up pains; I was a burden to them. They had their own worries.

All I knew was that what that teacher did was not right. I was determined more than ever to succeed. I knew that I would work very hard to make some money. In this way, I thought I would have some power. I realized as a young man that those with the dough have rights … the power of the purse. Those with the money are heard and because of their economic standing in the community, their kids had special rights that my family didn't have. What I did have in common with my siblings was tenacity and drive to work hard, and to be disciplined to put shelter over our heads and food on the table.

My pockets were empty and my heart was hurt. I didn't cry; I took another day in stride. Buck up, buster, you'll figure something out … a next move in your life.

In 1967, I was drafted in to the US Army. Unlike many I had a two year all-expense paid vacation. Food, clothing, and shelter was provided while stationed in Augsburg, Germany.

While I was in the army, I had lot of opportunity to think about my high school grades which had limited my choices. I took advantage of my time in Europe and since 1967, I have been traveling back and forth to Paris.

Today, I travel in style back and forth to Paris, I travel with my wife Pascale.

Once out of the army, I enrolled in college and graduated from USF funded by the GI Bill, and doubled my high school grade point average and graduated from USF with a 3.2 GPA, B.S. in Marketing and Accounting.

"It is never too late!"

I was committed to soar like an eagle but I had lots of work to do. Even with a college diploma, I had much work to make up for the lost opportunity as a student at Hudson's Bay High School.

I have learned that it is never too late.

To this day, I am committed to personal growth and development.

While I may not have contributed much to my classmates growing up, because of my rock 'n roll attitude. I am grateful to be here today.

After I received my diploma from the University of San Francisco, I returned to my high school to thank Mr. Jackson and Mr. Suckling for the time they had spent with me during my high school days. Also, I wanted to apologize to them for being a bad student and a bad boy, and to let them know that I had found my way. As I entered the school house, looking for Mr. Jackson and Mr. Suckling, I passed by the many trophy cases reminding me of many missed opportunities on the athletic field. This was my first visit to the school since graduation in 1965.

Immediately, as I entered the school reception office, I was greeted and put on the witness stand by Mrs. Richardson, one of the school counselors. I remembered her from my high school days. This day led to an encounter that I'll never forget. Mrs. Richardson asked me why I was at school. Uh-oh, I thought, I'm on the witness stand. If I want a hall pass to accomplish my mission, I would need to schmooze with her. I shared with her, using a courteous tone that I would like to visit with Mr. Jackson and Mr. Suckling. I went on to add, in my conversation with Mrs. Richardson, in my attempt at finding some warmth and a few kudos, that I had been drafted into the US Army after high school, and with the GI Bill, I had recently graduated from the University of San Francisco. She commented, with a telling tag in her voice, "Oh, you are a late bloomer."

Mr. Jackson and Mr. Suckling greeted me and gave me words of encouragement. I left with positive feelings. The men were full of support, encouragement, cordial, and very friendly, and I am glad to this day that I made the effort to thank them. They are good people; we need more teachers like these two guys.

It is never too late to the right thing.

After college graduation I became a stockbroker with Dean Witter & Co., now Morgan Stanley. While I enjoyed the work, I was pulled to become an entrepreneur. I wanted to paddle my own canoe.

In 1974, I launched Beards Frames, Frame Central Stores, Art Galleries, and production and distribution facilities for the following 25 years. Again, in 2001, I was hit with the entrepreneur bug, and jumped into the internet and launched another retail company, and most recently I am building a software solution company in the information management space.

On the personal side, since high school I have become a voracious reader of biographies studying the lives of people who have made a difference, I have been a serious student of French.

In learning to speak the French language, I met my wife Pascale.

In 1989, I began taking dancing lessons.

In 1993, joined Rotary.

"It is never too late."

In 2001, I joined a Toastmaster Club in Portland, and again …

"It is never too late."

From the days in high school, when I was shy and bashful, I am frequently on my feet to speak. Finding ones voice is one of the greatest legacies that we can leave to our children. When we find our voices they'll find theirs.

Even with some work to do in the personal growth and development department in front of me, I was focused on overcoming stage fright, and to do so I recognized that I needed to commit to attending Toastmasters every Thursday at 7:15 am.

"It is never too late."

With the encouragement from Clinical Psychologist Dr. Richard to learn French, I thought, why not … pourquoi pas.

It is never too late!

I had an opportunity to study French at HBHS, but I thought in high school this French stuff is not for me. After all, I was too busy working as a cashier and selling beer out of the backdoor at Park 'n Shop.

This is all before I met my best pal, my gal Pascale.

It takes a village to grow and develop a person. Each of us has more to learn and personal issues to work through.

It is never too late. I'm still in school.

My gal Pascale, my best pal, my best professeur, thank you for your love, support, and encouragement.

Pascale, as the years have flown by, your kind words before I left early in the mornings for Toastmasters or after work going to give a speech at a French class, your inspiration is just what I needed … encouragement.

On a more serious and provocative note, I have been rewarded through my French speaking classes and Toastmasters experiences with the ability to speak while on my feet.

"It is never too late."

Fellow Frenchman Louis Pasteur said, "Chance favors the prepared mind." When you have developed the ability to speak on your feet, you are ready wherever you go and whenever go. The world opens up to us.

We can have it all, all we need to do is the work.

"It is never too late."

I'm having fun and the best is yet to come. Thank you, thanks to all of you, for opportunity to connect with so many wonderful people.

While it may have taken me a little longer than many of you,

"It is never too late."

Linda Clark … fellow classmates!

Let's not wait another 50 years to have another reunion it might be too late!

Ending: "Now we may begin." Philip Roth

We can have it all, all we have to do is the work.

Reflection, Renewal, and Resilience

SEPTEMBER IS A TIME for new beginnings as the kids go back to school, to college, the evenings grow shorter, and we start anew at work following summer respite.

During our hiatus periods, we have time to think, to process and make sense out of what is happening in our world. I have had a lot to think about during my recent summer vacation. I have come to value the opportunity for reflection and renewal during summer break.

For me September is a very special time. Reflection and renewal and in several ways The New Year.

All too often we live frantic lives chasing success fueled on Starbucks. Reflection brings renewal. I stand before you today, the luckiest man alive, to borrow a page from Lou Gehrig, for an opportunity to reflect and grow in several ways for which I am grateful.

Each year, during September, I am reminded of my time at the Pendleton Round-up, in 1981, when I was in transition moving from marriage to singlehood. When I took the risk by going to Pendleton, I learned a lot about myself by meeting a wonderful lady named Julie, who challenged me to loosen up. Hence the speech which I gave a few years ago: Sweet & Salty.

In the years gone by during September, year after year, as a single father, I sent my two sons in different directions off to different cities and to colleges and until several years ago, I said my good-byes solo. These moments of departure have taught me the value of separateness and togetherness.

Like everyone, we are asked by family and friends, "how was your summer?" I respond, "Great!" On occasion I respond with the opportunity to do a deeper dive and share the real me.

The dog days of summer give birth to renewal to plumb the depths of what I will be doing going forward in the months ahead. Where do I want to be by this year end?

I am reminded of Erik Eriksen's life cycle steps each September. Life is about growth and development. The lessons that I learn though periods of crisis yield a bountiful harvest of opportunity.

Consciously on my mind, as I reflect, is Karen Horney, who was born in Hamburg, 1885, a psychologist who moved to NYC after she earned her degrees in Germany. She died in 1952, in NYC. Horney is known for her thoughts which are dear to me. When we move away from something what are we moving toward? We do it consciously or unconsciously the choice is ours to make.

My younger son is off to his final term at UCB. This September send-off will be my last with him before his next chapter unfolds.

This September, my wife Pascale is off to Paris to be with her mother, my wonderful mother-in-law, who lives in assisted living just north of Paris. Togetherness and separation.

Consciously. Each September, I move from an old place to a new space to that of renewal.

This September, I have moved along to new opportunities that I wasn't expecting. I welcome the opportunity to go where it feels good, to swim in another pool where the waters might be a little warmer.

This year, during the dog days of summer, I have had an experience which will go down in my diary, a life sculpting event, that has delivered puzzling consequences. How was I dealt these cards? I reflect.

A couple of experiences parallel each other, second homes. This summer, I emptied out my mother-in-law's apartment in Paris, it was base camp for our second home in Paris. Family dinners. She spent more than 60 plus years of her now 88 years in the same apartment. However, it took less than 60 minutes to clean out the apartment. I was wondering how can one live in an apartment that long and to have it all go away so fast. What is the meaning of those sixty years that evaporated so fast? The memories will last but the second home is history. She didn't plan her exit. She didn't listen to Karen Horney's advice, she unconsciously and unwillingly moved toward and landed in assisted living. For her there is no going back. For me there is no going back. We take the cherished memories and we create anew, a renewal, with an eye to consciously design the future.

Last year, in September, I lost a friend of many years. It is his passing, that has reminded me of my own mortality and how I could make a difference in this world, like my friend did for so many years. I have the memories but things are different for me now when I go to Santa Cruz. I have taken the time for renewal.

Years ago, in the summer of 2006, after a brush with death, I came back to AC Toastmasters in September, a new man, one who took a time out, on a have to basis, renewal was a must.

I have been through like many of you, through the tough times and the good times. What I share with you today, in the process of my September renewals is what I do to make sure that my childlike spirit is alive and will not be squelched.

There is something about this summer which has given me eyes to see like no other. It is during the tough times that we learn who are our real friends, who are our buddies, and who are mere acquaintances. But a handful are true allies. This discovery is a gift bestowed only by those who have navigated stormy seas and survived.

Each and every time that I have been hit with a curve ball or a bean ball, I have landed on a higher step, guided by reading about and learning from Karen Horney, Marie Curie, and Nietzsche. What doesn't kill us makes us stronger.

Through the loss of loved ones, through reducing the size of one's family, working through financial struggles, and living through a major health issue or getting on the wrong short list, or losing a second home, I consider myself to be the luckiest man in the world. It is the tough stuff which is handled properly which gives us a growth spurt like no other. There is a price for being an outlier, but I love it. It makes my heart sing.

After a period of reflection and renewal during the summer Toastmaster vacation, I return and I am reminded of the wonderful gifts which you have all given me and to each other. Yes. It is here where I have found my voice, in this room, in this building. It took this club, this village, all of you for me to be so proud to be a part of this wonderful organization.

This Toastmaster Club has spawned another Toastmasters Club that is becoming the heart soul of the Portland Rotary Club. Since last September, the Portland Rotary Toastmaster Club has grown in exponential proportions and we are helping others to find their voices.

Thank you all for what you have done and continue to do to make this a better world.

Becoming a Self-Made Man:

Flight to Paradise

It is difficult to scramble to have a life, to blast through self-made obstacles, but now I'm beginning to live life in paradise. Why? I'm living life my way!

With head down, for most of my life, I was constantly wriggling my way out of the poor house but I had no idea that I needed to create a life once I escaped the bonds of poverty. Work was all I knew. I had not built a Renaissance life that later I would find and develop through unlearning earlier poisonous pedagogy and making and creating a new life with positive, possibility thinking.

In meeting Dr. Richard, I began the long trek to freedom through his pedagogy, encouragement, support and empowerment. First, I needed lots of help to find my identity. Prior to meeting Dr. Richard, I had always laid out the wrong welcome mat; "It is okay to be toxic with me." I had been squelched and shut down, I had been labeled a bad boy and I had lived up to that image that I wasn't good enough.

One of the first steps when I was "ready" was to sell the companies which I founded. Why? My parents and siblings had as minority stockholders a stranglehold of control over me, not only held hostage by the laws which protect minority shareholders but emotionally I had to meet them on their terms.

In 1999, I sold the controlling interest in the companies to some well-financed and sharp people in Seattle, Washington. When I received a nice payday for working around the clock for more than 30 years, little did I know then that in my early 50's, I was just beginning to find my identity.

Even though I had been working with Dr. Richard more than 12 years, finally, all that I had been learning from him through therapy sessions and reading many books, I was starting to feel the evolution of moving from an old small world to a new bigger, and better world.

After selling my interest in my namesake companies, and now with a few dollars in my pocket and no desire to retire, I was looking to find what would make me happy. How do I define happiness?

I invested small amounts in several companies, with mediocre returns. Getting involved in start-ups is not always a freeway paved with gold. I invested in one company that took a chunk out of my pocket. The consequences of this decision have caused me to take inventory and to take stock of who I am, what I want to become and importantly who would I like to become.

Looking back, I have come to realize that I have spent countless hours during the last nearly twenty years learning how to speak, French, improve my English writing skills and over the last thirteen years my public speaking skills.

A firm handshake and a clear and expressive signature were tools which I had cultivated and am very proud of as they provide me with a distinctive brand. Little by little, I was claiming me. In my early forties, I went to the courthouse and jettisoned my slave name "Terrill" and changed my ID to my nickname "Terry." Once I changed my name, my signature evolved and I felt better about me. I had decided for myself that now I was on my way to developing my rules of the road. This day in court changing my name was the beginning of the breaking of my lease on the uncivilized world, which I had been chained to.

Now I was ready to move from alienation to integration. I was flying under Terry's flag, my own brand. The name Terrill, indeed was a reminder that I was a boy unwanted because my mother wanted a daughter named Cheryl. I was no longer living life on anyone's else's terms by default.

When I started on my quest it was an unconscious quest to become a better student in life and today, I have found my niche.

The number one thing that most people fear is now what gets my mo'jo going!

I like to tell stories, I like to entertain with my storytelling, and I like to encourage others to conquer their fears and get up on their feet and speak.

Through my style of public speaking, through storytelling, I have found myself at the table among captains of industry, and community leaders, who want to share friendship and what life fully has to offer. Many have accomplished much but fall into a trap of complacency, a rut straight to the grave. As readers hear my stories about wriggling free from the cages of the clipped wing society, hopefully much of what I talk about will resonate with them.

Through speech craft, I have found that through opening up and the sharing of myself, I can encourage others. I have a deep, deep understanding of myself and a lust to share that understanding with others to help jumpstart them.

We can all fly high if we do the work of claiming ourselves—C'est moi!

Part IV

Letters to My Sons

Passing the Torch to the Next Generation

To My Older Son Jeff

(Departing for Rotary Leadership Camp, July 1996)

Dear Jeff,

Today, I am the luckiest man in the world. I have been asked to share a few words about what I find so wonderful about you. The Leadership of Rotary Youth Leadership Awards Camp has knocked at the door of opportunity. I welcome and embrace the occasion to answer the knock by thanking you and thanking them for celebrating you. Let's take a peek inside a very special guy.

In 1976, our country celebrated 200 years as a Nation. I was with you on that very sunny day, the 20th of May … your Birthday. Life has never been the same…the sunshine that you brought to me that day continues to radiate a life full of hopes and dreams which I have for you. Celebrating in 1976 was a double bonus year. We were shooting off firecrackers in celebration of our country's 200th Birthday and I was asking myself some questions about my duties and responsibilities as your father. How do I contribute to the hopes and dreams not only of our country but to the hopes and dreams of someone who will represent the future of this country … a future leader.

Jeff, it warms my heart and brings tears to my eyes, as I think back over the years about how hard I worked to create a better life for you. You understood at an early age the need for your Mother and me to work hard. You were and are today most appreciative of our labors. You and I were always there for each other when I got home from work. We played for hours after work until it was "beddy bye time" … you would be waiting for me in the "jumping johnny" suspended in the kitchen doorway. Frequently, we would do a little boating together in the big tub … "rub a dub dub … two men in a tub."

Your beautiful and sparkling eyes communicated in those early years, as they communicate today, your warm heart, your fantastic sense of humor, your high level of intelligence, and your ability to bring people in close to be with you … to play, laugh and giggle.

On March 4, 1980, early on a Friday afternoon, my divorce from your Mother decreed that it was moving day; you drove with your mom to San Diego. I will never forget that day. You and your Mom stopped outside the office along Macadam Avenue to wave "good-bye." I was young then … going on 34 years. The time passed and it did ever so slowly. Jeff, you were now living in San Diego. We didn't have our time to snuggle, to be together or to play with your Hot Wheels in the driveway, but six weeks later, I arrived in San Diego, and we began our adventure of commuting between Portland and San Diego that would last nearly 15 years. On my first trip to San Diego I was greeted at the airport by you with a squirt gun in hand and a little water in the eye and asked if we were going to Disneyland. I knew the answer … and we had a blast!

The most important decision of my life was made on my first trip to visit you in San Diego. I would return frequently to San Diego to be with you. Each time I arrived in San Diego, I was greeted with your enthusiasm to see me, to share your life and my eagerness to see what you were up to. We moved from squirt guns, to skateboards … collecting baseball cards, going to Padres games, to the World Series, to the Super Bowl, playing basketball together … Cub Scouts, Little League, Pony League, football, meeting the gals, high school dances, a little PTA, out with your buddies, doing a little studying … walking along the coast in the village of Del Mar sharing and developing a philosophy about life … about the value of making friends, skiing together, and going to lots of dinners together at The Fishmarket on Jimmy Durante Boulevard. We went to a few museums, went to SeaWorld on a regular basis to have Shamu and Mamu give us a bath as they splashed water out of the big pools. We have been to hundreds of movies together never to miss an opportunity to share lots of popcorn dripping with hot butter. Along with you, you gave me the opportunity to have my childhood … too!

The times that I would tuck you in and say goodnight to you over the phone from Portland made things go better for both of us. However, I want to thank you Jeff for all the time we spent together in San Diego and Portland … we had a long distance relationship in legal address only … we lived up close … real close to each other, we didn't accept the landscape distance between us as an issue or a problem. The only turbulence we experienced was the choppy air at times between Portland and San Diego.

The challenge of divorce was not an obstacle to our building an incredible relationship. We made the commitment to build our relationship despite the distance and today … yes, I am the luckiest guy in the world. I am proud to be your father … and those 15 years will always be remembered as years that have not only contributed to your growth but to mine as well. We made the right choices. We traveled back and forth for nearly 15 years between our two cities, and the hopes and dreams that I had for you, in 1976, have already spawned a bountiful harvest.

Every day, I think about my favorite guy who is full of love, and la joie de vivre. I think about what it means to have the wonderful opportunity to be your father. Frequently, I ask myself what is it that I can pass on to you as a lasting gift … a gift to leave behind that best exemplifies my love for you.

One of the greatest legacies that I can leave behind is the enduring gift of that heritage which you can take indoors and make your own. The teaching that I share in word and deed represents a loving pedagogy … involving the importance of values, personal guidelines and a moral compass which will equip you to take your place in the world as a competent and caring citizen. My commitment to this effort and accomplishment, pursued conscientiously, is an important part of the hope for a better tomorrow...for you, us, and *tout le monde.*

Being your Dad is both fun and serious work as a result of the important stakes at issue. Teaching in the context of fun and goodwill seems to yield the best results. We have our outdoor playground with a basketball net where we do most of our outdoor work which we take indoors. (Sometimes, the rain showers send us back into the nearby family room... before the game is finished but we continue to do our outdoor work indoors.) Thanks for asking me out daily to the basketball hoop in our front yard...where we grow and play together in our garden of fun, learning and wisdom. I not only enjoy it but I am proud and happy to be a big part of the development of my super star on our home court and out in the arena of life. It is great fun for me to be witnessing the positive contributions that you are already making in creating a better world…with more to come.

An awesome challenge … and a task it is. You make it fun and the work seems and feels like play. Thanks, Big Guy! Occasionally, when I have had to work a little overtime at being a parent … I always felt better and re-energized because you always have given and continue to give me the time to accept guidance and direction graciously … with a little nudging along the path of wisdom. I am glad that I have undertaken the challenges as your father…the response and the results are tremendous.

It is my job to share with you the menu of life and its opportunities.

You amaze me at how well you engage the doing … your ability to shake hands with the doing is tooling you up for this world to be a leader in the new millennium. You are guided by high standards and values which cause people to look up to you in awe with admiration. You have learned that the choices you make will sculpt your world and will impact those around and with you. Jeff, you motivate and inspire me to do my work … to continue to do my own personal growth. We truly have cultivated an aerobics plan that has us off our butts and on to the dance floor of life … doing the doing! The music sounds and feels wonderful!

Jeff … you are a warm and caring person, coupled with a fantastic sense of humor which magnetizes everyone with whom you touch. People like and enjoy you big time. You are guided by the Dale Carnegie Principles of how to make friends and be friends … and from the Dale Carnegie School, you have become an accomplished public speaker.

You are a wonderful big brother to your little brother Gabriel. He couldn't ask for a better and more loving brother. He looks up to you, loves you and watches the clock knowing that you are coming to town to spend time with him … he is following in your footsteps. Jeff, he has developed rapidly because of your leadership, genuine love and care for him. Gabriel, at 10 years of age, has learned from you the importance and the differences between scholarship and sports and their place in this world. Recently with your big brotherly gentle insistence he is well into digesting Carnegie's book, *How to Win Friends and Influence People*. As he reads along, he reminds me of you. He is asking lots of questions and looking up words he doesn't know with a dictionary ... our Book Smart bookmark vocabulary list we created together in 1992, around a campfire in Central Oregon.

Frequently, I write little notes to you and leave them on the kitchen counter ... and today, I enjoy leaving these notes not only in English but in our second language French ... the most beautiful language in the world ... ooh-la-la! Your ability to work and study hard ... is one of your great strengths. As you continue to travel the world ... your knowledge of another language will not only open doors and windows of opportunity but will generate more goodwill for all of us. The French language is the language of relationships and diplomacy. It is an opportunity for us to have private conversations in public in downtown Portland as we do often.

Your ability to understand that the choices that you make will not only sculpt your life and that of others but will shape for you the life that you will live and leave behind.

Jeff, you are guided by a high functioning value system ... which clearly exhibits leadership qualities and skills that will take you far in this world. With your passion, enthusiasm, wisdom, and insight for living, you are creating a world full of promise for yourself and to gift others.

You have a handle on a priority system that will save you time...that you will take you further down the road moving forward rather than spending unnecessary time constantly digging yourself out of holes ... you have the tools and continue to sharpen them ... to live on the cutting edge.

You continue to appreciate the value of reaching out and learning to do new things ... making life an adventure and a journey, and one day the whole world will be reading about you on the best seller list ... the guy who did it all, a Renaissance Man. A Man with a mission and a sense of purpose who lives and lived life to the fullest ... "and left the world a little better than he found it." (Dr. Richard)

Jeff, you have it all. You remind me each and every day that as I have learned from Louis Pasteur that "chance favors the prepared mind." We have a hobby ... one we share ... questing and taking all the good stuff in from the people who have lived to make a difference ... you study as I do what the "questers" do, have done and continue to do … like Albert Einstein, Franklin, Eleanor, and Theodore Roosevelt, Pierre and Marie Curie, Benjamin Franklin, Dr. Richard, Abraham Lincoln, George Washington Carver, George Washington, Paul Harris, Winston Churchill, Charles Darwin, and many others ….

In 1994, you became an Oregon resident, and enrolled at the U of O. Jeff thanks for moving to Oregon. Today, we have the best of all worlds. We live near each other, the travel time has been lessened considerably, and we visit with each other frequently. We still laugh and play together big time…the conversation today gets my mojo workin' with excitement as I see your lust for life soaring to new and higher heights. In the last few years, your commitment to working and studying hard at college coupled with your quest for personal growth will create for you a legacy that you lived to make a difference.

Jeff, you make my job as a father, the most enjoyable thing I have ever done. I celebrate you and for what you are and are becoming … a Renaissance Man. You are a Renaissance man with a lust for life who enjoys living a full-spectrum lifestyle … questing, reaching, developing, growing, connecting … traveling and zooming towards new horizons with zest and gusto … life is a treasure hunt for you. You strive to be all that you can be … to share with family, friends, and colleagues … to have the best people as mentors to learn from and in turn share the opportunities with others … to be an exemplar, a leader in living life by design and created through full-spectrum living that you can have it all … all you have to do is the work … and in doing so you are already making a difference at home, at work, and at play.

Thanks Jeff for always making the time to powwow over lunch and dinner. Once we have ordered off the restaurant menu and sorted through the wine list we take the time to study our own menus. Thanks for liking the big deep red wines. Our own menu, as we know, are on-going thoughts and ideas which we have scribbled on little jotters gifted to us from Dr. Richard. Jeff, I am amazed at what we have talked about and shared. Your ability to process and develop an Operating Manifesto comes with a Table of Contents which is noteworthy.

We have surfed through life and clarified the way we would like to design it from the value of creating a family by accident to reaching out and creating one on purpose … love … friends … career, religion, money, environment, relationships, good books to read, learning new words together, community service, service above self, fellowship, humor and its value, values, celebration, taking, risks, giving oral book reports, health, exercise, choices, education, thank you notes, birthday cards, traveling the world, our choice of words … our linguistic personalities.

Living life conscientiously, priorities, time management, and what you do between 5 and 10 p.m. will more than likely determine who you will be and the level of contribution you will make in this world … and that spontaneity and variety is the spice of life and there are a few more roads left for us to journey.

Jeff, I am reminded of a dream that I had. It was so impacting that I had it scripted suitable for framing … framed to celebrate our incredible relationship.

The magnificent legacy that I will leave behind in the form of you moral competence and the good moral fiber in you is the greatest gift and reward of all. This is the joy of my parenting efforts.

Jeff, I look forward to living to be a 100 that I may be able to have The Galilean View I dreamed of a few years ago.

Love,
Dad

My Best Dream… 21 August 1990, in Paris

(Musing about my son Jeff)

Jeff,

You and I are walking along and all of sudden you begin to cry.

"Jeff, why are you crying?"

"Dad, I like holding hands, but I would rather sit on your shoulders, so I can see more."

"Jeff, I want you to stand on my shoulders, so you can see even more."

"Okay, Dad."

"Jeff, will you tell me everything you see standing on my shoulders?"

"Dad, I will tell you everything!"

"Thanks."

"Hey, Dad it is really neat up here, thanks!"

I love you, I celebrate you, and I am there for you. I pass the torch of enlightenment to your capable hands and I can rest easy knowing that the new millennium will be in the care and custody of your capable stewardship. *Carpe Diem!!*

Love,

Dad

To My Two Sons

(Father's Day 1997)

Dear Jeff and Gabriel,

Every day, I think about my two favorite guys who are full of love, and *la joie de vivre*. I think about what it means to have the wonderful opportunity to be your father. Frequently, I ask myself what is it that I can pass on to you as a lasting gift … a gift to leave behind that best exemplifies my love for you.

One of the greatest gifts that I can leave behind is the enduring gift of that heritage which you can take indoors and make your own. The teaching that I share in word and deed represents a loving pedagogy … involving the importance of values, personal guidelines and a moral compass which will equip you guys to take your places in the world as competent and caring citizens. My commitment to this effort and accomplishment, pursued conscientiously, is an important part of the hope for a better tomorrow … for you, us, and *tout le monde*.

Being your Dad is both fun and serious work as a result of the important stakes at issue. Teaching in the context of fun and goodwill seems to yield the best results. We have our outdoor playground with a basketball net where we do most of our outdoor work which we then take indoors. (Sometimes, the rain showers send us back into the nearby family room … before the game is finished but we continue to do our outdoor work indoors.) Thanks for asking me out daily to the basketball hoop in our front yard…where we grow and play together in our garden of fun, learning and wisdom. I not only enjoy it, playing with you guys, but I am proud and happy to be a big part of the development of my two superstars on our home court and out in the university of life. It is great fun for me to be witnessing the positive contributions that you are already making in creating a better world…with more to come.

The magnificent legacy that I will leave behind in the form of your moral competence and the good moral fiber in you is the greatest gift and reward of all. This is the joy of my parenting efforts.

I love you, I celebrate you, and I am there for you,
Dad

P.S. It is my job to help you find your passion, not to tell you what your passion is or should be!

Epilogue: Wheels Down

It has been a long journey, but the runway is in sight and touch down on the tarmac is imminent.

Dear readers, thank you for flying with me during this long journey with many stops and starts, turbulence, and emergency landings along the way. It has been an exciting journey, a fruitful journey during which I have shed lots of baggage so that I might fly higher and soar with eagles.

I hope that some of the lessons which emerge from my long flight to freedom will be helpful to you as you assemble your own flight manual.

You can manage your own flight to freedom as long as you assemble your own flight manual.

I have worked long and hard over the years to be able to fly with my own wings. You can do it also; all you have to do is the work.

The formula is in front of your nose as you get ready to wriggle through the bars of the cage that has kept you grounded. I invite you to come fly with me. See you in the Stratosphere!—The end and the beginning.

—Terry Beard

PRAISE FOR SQUELCHED

Awareness by awareness, discovery by discovery, fueled by true grit and resolve Terry snipped away the tethers of the past and created his own opportunity to soar to new heights and fly with the eagles.

—Dr. Richard, Professor of Psychology at Portland Community College, Portland, Oregon, USA

Terry's enthusiasm has helped countless men and women "find their voice". The book is refreshingly honest and enjoyable to read. Terry's storytelling throughout the book will motivate others to seek their potential. I hope you enjoy the book as much as I did.

—Al Jubitz, President, Jubitz Family Foundation, Portland, Oregon, USA, Investing in Children, the Environment, and Peace

Terry Beard has written an inspiring memoir that will serve as an example of how to achieve success regardless of your circumstances. His stories will warm your heart and make you laugh and help you find your voice.

—Gary Schmidt Clackamas, Oregon, USA, Past International President, Toastmasters International 2009-2010

When I read *Squelched* one year ago I was on the way to change my life. It made me realize that when you need to do something important it is possible although it seems so difficult. It is very frightening but it is possible! For me it was amazing to read Terry's story, he has done so much in his life and I admire him for that. What I also appreciate with Terry is his interest in other people.

—Susanne Millien, Ydre, Sweden, and Paris, France, The Swedish Circle

Squelched: Finding My Voice is the story of anyone's journey, male or female. If you came of age with never-ending scripts from parents, teachers, friends, and others saying, "You can't…" "you shouldn't…" and "you won't…" this is for you. Terry Beard learned he could and he should… then he DID. He tells his story with honesty, humility, and humor, drawing you in with a writing style that allows you to find your story. I recommend *Squelched* to clients who ask: "Should I…?" "Can I…?" "Will I…?" Then I ask, "Why shouldn't you…?" "Why can't you…?" and "Why wouldn't you?"
—Susan Goldstein, Navigating Professional & Organizational
Contours, Portland, Oregon, USA